Socioeconomic

Impacts

of Water

Conservation

The mission of the AWWA Research Foundation (AWWARF) is to advance the science of water to improve the quality of life. Funded primarily through annual subscription payments from over 1,000 utilities, consulting firms, and manufacturers in North America and abroad, AWWARF sponsors research on all aspects of drinking water, including supply and resources, treatment, monitoring and analysis, distribution, management, and health effects.

From its headquarters in Denver, Colorado, the AWWARF staff directs and supports the efforts of over 500 volunteers, who are the heart of the research program. These volunteers, serving on various boards and committees, use their expertise to select and monitor research studies to benefit the entire drinking water community.

Research findings are disseminated through a number of technology transfer activities, including research reports, conferences, videotape summaries, and periodicals.

Socioeconomic Impacts of Water Conservation

Janice A. Beecher
Beecher Policy Research, Inc.
6225 Vancouver Court
Indianapolis, IN 46236

Thomas W. Chesnutt
A & N Technical Services, Inc.
839 Second Street, Suite 5
Encinitas, CA 92024

David M. Pekelney
A & N Technical Services, Inc.
2450 20th Street, Suite F
Santa Monica, CA 90405

AWWA Research Foundation
6666 W. Quincy Avenue
Denver, CO 80235-3098

Published by the
AWWA Research Foundation and
American Water Works Association

DISCLAIMER

This study was funded by the AWWA Research Foundation (AWWARF). AWWARF assumes no responsibility for the content of the research study reported in this publication or for the opinions or statements of fact expressed in the report. The mention of trade names for commercial products does not represent or imply the approval or endorsement of AWWARF. This report is presented solely for informational purposes.

Library of Congress Cataloging-in-Publication Data

Beecher, Janice A.
    Socioeconomic impact of water conservation / prepared by Janice A. Beecher,
Thomas W. Chesnutt, David M. Pekelney ; sponsored by AWWA Research Foundation.
        p. cm.
    Includes bibliographical references.
    ISBN 1-58321-078-4
    1. Water utilities. 2. Water conservation--Economic aspects. I. Chesnutt, Thomas W.
II. Pekelney, David M. III. AWWA Research Foundation. IV. Title.

HD4456.B44 2000
333.91'16--dc21   00-046902

Printed on recycled paper.

CONTENTS

TABLES

FIGURES

FOREWORD

The AWWA Research Foundation is a nonprofit corporation dedicated to the implementation of a research effort to help utilities respond to regulatory requirements and traditional high-priority concerns of the industry. The research agenda is developed through a process of consultation with subscribers and drinking-water professionals. Under the umbrella of a Strategic Research Plan, the Research Advisory Council prioritizes the suggested projects based upon current and future needs, applicability, and past work; the recommendations are forwarded to the Board of Trustees for final selection. The foundation also sponsors research projects through the unsolicited proposal process; the Collaborative Research, Research Applications, and Tailored Collaboration programs; and various joint research efforts with organizations such as the U.S. Environmental Protection Agency, the U.S. Bureau of Reclamation, and the Association of California Water Agencies.

This publication is a result of one of these sponsored studies, and it is hoped that its findings will be applied in communities throughout the world. The report serves not only as a means of communicating the results of the water industry's centralized research program but also as a tool to enlist further support of the nonmember utilities and individuals.

Projects are managed closely from their inception to the final report by the foundation's staff and large cadre of volunteers who willingly contribute their time and expertise. The foundation serves a planning and management function and awards contracts to other institutions such as water utilities, universities, and engineering firms. Funding for this research effort comes primarily from the Subscription Program, through which water utilities subscribe to the research program and make an annual payment proportionate to the volume of water they deliver, and consultants and manufacturers subscribe based on their annual billings. The program offers a cost-effective and fair method for funding research in the public interest.

A broad spectrum of water supply issues is addressed by the foundation's research agenda: resources, treatment and operations, distribution and storage, water quality and analysis, toxicology, economics, and management. The ultimate purpose of the coordinated effort is to assist water suppliers to provide the highest possible quality of water economically and reliably. The true benefits are realized when the results are implemented at the utility level. The foundation's trustees are pleased to offer this publication as a contribution toward that end.

Water conservation programs have proliferated over the years because of limited high-quality water resources, costs of expanding water treatment facilities, and an increasingly conservation-minded water supply industry. The impacts of water conservation programs on drinking water utility customers, however, has not been assessed comprehensively from a socioeconomic viewpoint. This report explores the interrelationship between water conservation programs and socioeconomic characteristics and impacts. Specifically, the report summarizes an investigation of (1) the socioeconomic characteristics of utility customers and water use, (2) the socioeconomic impacts of conservation programs, and (3) the effectiveness of conservation programs in terms of socioeconomic impacts.

Julius Ciaccia, Jr.

Chair, Board of Trustees

AWWA Research Foundation

James F. Manwaring, P.E.

Executive Director

AWWA Research Foundation

ACKNOWLEDGMENTS

The authors of this report express gratitude to the following water utilities and their personnel that contributed their expertise, experience, and data to this research effort:

Los Angeles Department of Water and Power: Tom Gackstetter, George Martin, and Margaret Pollyea

Phoenix Water Services Department: Thomas Babcock, Jane Ploeser, and Jeff DeWitt

City of Portland (Oregon) Bureau of Water Works: Cindy Dietz and James Burke

St. Louis County Water Company: Kent Turner, James Jenkins, Thomas Deters, and Rita Scott

The authors also gratefully acknowledge the members of the Project Advisory Committee: Mary Ann Dickinson, Scott Rubin, and Christopher Woodcock. Finally, the authors thank Dr. Charles Matzke, Beecher Policy Research, Inc., for research assistance related to this project. The authors especially appreciate the advice and guidance of the AWWA Research Foundation project manager, Robert Allen.

EXECUTIVE SUMMARY

In the design and implementation of utility policies and programs, socioeconomic impacts on the service area population often are ignored or given little attention. But ignoring these impacts—the unintended effects of conservation programs—has analytical, practical, and political consequences. At the same time, socioeconomic characteristics of the service area population are often ignored or given little attention.

RESEARCH OBJECTIVES

The following are the objectives of this report:

- To perform valid, insightful, and well-documented case studies of conservation programs at four water utilities
- To demonstrate methods that utility managers can use to quantitatively depict the financial effects of conservation programs on low-income households and utility finances
- To identify and explain innovative conservation programs targeting low-income customers, their effects and prospects
- To provide concrete guidance for managers to design and implement conservation programs to address equity and utility finance issues

APPROACH

This report explores the interrelationship between water conservation programs and socioeconomic characteristics and impacts. The conceptual approach represents three questions (chapter 2). First, how do socioeconomic characteristics of utility customers affect water use and conservation, independently of utility programs and activities? Second, in what ways do utility programs and activities (including pricing changes) have socioeconomic impacts on utility customers (especially their income)? Third, how do socioeconomic characteristics of utility customers influence the effectiveness of utility programs and activities in terms of water use and conservation? Addressing these issues can help water utility managers design more effective programs.

Several in-depth case studies were conducted to identify innovative utility programs that consider socioeconomic conditions, particularly income, in their program design. A formal interview protocol was developed and revised to guide the information collection. The utility participants who shared their experiences, insight, and knowledge in this study are

- Los Angeles Department of Water and Power
- Phoenix Water Department
- City of Portland (Oregon) Bureau of Water Works
- St. Louis County Water Company

The interview protocol and case study summaries can be found in Appendix A. The experiences of several other utilities that have included conservation elements in programs to assist low-income and other customer groups also are described (chapter 5). The available evaluation studies of select utility experiences with targeted water conservation programs generally report positive utility experiences and results. With few exceptions, water savings and cost savings that directly benefit the targeted population are achieved. Assistance programs including a conservation component also report positive results.

FINDINGS

How does socioeconomics affect water use?

Water use varies according to income, household size, age, gender, region, ethnicity, employment, education, and other characteristics (chapter 3). Water demand modeling highlights the relevance and relative importance of socioeconomic characteristics in explaining water use. Water use is a function of a number of key variables, specifically: population, climate and weather (temperature and rainfall), price (average and marginal), and socioeconomic characteristics (including income). Income is a particularly important determinant of water use. Generally, higher income households are expected to use more water. Low-income households may present opportunities for water savings that will translate into improved affordability.

How do utility programs have socioeconomic consequences?

As already introduced, water utility programs—including pricing—have socioeconomic consequences. In particular, pricing and other deliberative actions by utilities can affect household income. That is, pricing methods and other programs can have distributional effects that make some households better off and some households worse off by affecting the prices paid for water service and for participating in utility programs. Although these effects typically are measured in terms of income, other metrics (such as consumer attitudes) also can be used to assess impacts. A framework for assessing the conservation, pricing, and affordability is presented (chapter 4).

How should utilities incorporate socioeconomic considerations?

Planners and policy makers can use a decision framework to jointly consider economic, equity, and other criteria in fulfilling their goals (chapter 6). Existing analytic methods, such as benefit-cost analysis or cost-effectiveness analysis, can be adapted for the purpose of under-standing the socioeconomic impacts of conservation programs and how knowledge of socioeco-nomic characteristics can improve planning. Using the broader policy analysis framework can be an effective way to systematically organize decision making without relying exclusively on an economic or any other single criterion. Several illustrations are used to explore the use of the analytical framework (chapter 7).

Rate design is no different from other water conservation programs in that it will have socioeconomic impacts and that these impacts can be assessed. Analytical methods used to eval-uate changes in rates and rate design also can be adapted to consider socioeconomic impacts. Price has direct and potentially significant impacts on one socioeconomic factor in particular: income. Even utilities without explicit conservation programs should consider the effect of price changes on water usage and on customers. The report provides an overview and illustration of tools for evaluating the effect of general and conservation-oriented price changes on water demand, utility revenues, and customers (chapter 8). All three of these variables have socioeconomic dimensions. Particular attention is paid to the evaluation of customer bill impacts.

CONCLUSION

Utilities can follow several available strategies to design programs that recognize and respond to socioeconomic conditions in the service territory. The report provides an overview of design and implementation issues for programs that simultaneously address water conservation and socioeconomic considerations (chapter 9). Water utilities can achieve conservation goals while also being responsive to socioeconomic considerations.

CHAPTER 1

SOCIOECONOMIC IMPACTS OF WATER CONSERVATION: AN INTRODUCTION

INTRODUCTION

The *socioeconomic characteristics* of a water utility's service area population are often ignored or paid little attention. Lack of data and a suitable framework for analysis may be to blame. In the design and implementation of utility policies and programs, *socioeconomic impacts* on the service area population also are frequently ignored or paid little attention. But neglecting these impacts—the unintended effects of conservation programs—has analytical, practical, and political consequences. Failing to recognize socioeconomic impacts of conservation programs and how socioeconomic characteristics influence program effectiveness can undermine program success, mask opportunities to realize savings, produce unintended consequences, ignore equity implications, and strain relationships with utility customers.

This report explores the interrelationships among socioeconomic characteristics, water conservation programs, and impacts. The intent is to provide water managers with practical information and guidance on how to consider socioeconomic impacts in the course of designing and implementing conservation and other utility programs.

PURPOSE

Water utilities implement water conservation programs to save water, to improve economic efficiency, and to reduce financial burdens on utilities and their customers. The definition of water conservation as a *beneficial* reduction in water use recognizes that conservation helps achieve water-use and efficiency goals. Most water utilities can realize benefits through supply-side and demand-side conservation measures, including conservation programs as well as conservation-oriented pricing. But the case for efficiency and conservation has been made elsewhere and need not be replicated here (see Chesnutt, McSpadden, and Christianson 1996).

Thus, the purpose of this report is not to provide a rationale for water conservation or water conservation planning. Nor is the purpose to convince utilities to adopt a program to address

1

affordability or other concerns that arise in the study of socioeconomic issues (see Saunders et al. 1998). Rather, the purpose of this report is to focus attention on the socioeconomic impacts of water conservation programs and the importance of understanding socioeconomic characteristics when designing and implementing such programs.

This research intends to meet unmet needs. Some policy analysts have acknowledged that socioeconomic issues often are overlooked in water conservation efforts (Babcock 1995). Yet, little clear theoretical or empirical guidance is available on the socioeconomic dimensions of water conservation. Nor can generalizations be easily made about how certain populations or subpopulations will behave in the context of a conservation program.

Utility managers can benefit by understanding the potential for socioeconomic conditions and characteristics to affect water use and conservation, and vice versa. This report provides background, case studies, and assessment tools for incorporating an understanding of socioeconomic issues into conservation planning and conservation-oriented pricing. The report is written to be useful for conservation managers, as well as for utility managers involved in rate setting, public education, and customer-assistance programs.

This report begins with the premise that the utility manager *already* implements or wants to implement some conservation measures. These measures might range from a modest consumer-education program to an efficiency-oriented rate structure to a plumbing-fixture rebate program. The conservation measures need not be part of a comprehensive or an aggressive conservation program. Indeed, some measures might be implemented only in the context of other utility programs, such as educational or assistance efforts.

Various water conservation activities implemented by water utilities affect people in ways that depend on their socioeconomic characteristics. The premise of the report is that the efficacy of conservation activities, and the cost effectiveness of conservation programs, can be enhanced greatly by an understanding of how these socioeconomic characteristics come into play. Water conservation cannot simply be *imposed* on customers, because water conservation involves human dispositions and behaviors; customer understanding, support, and cooperation are essential to effective water conservation efforts (City of Phoenix 1998). It follows that water conservation programs should recognize the role of these factors.

2

APPROACH

A challenge for this research is the potential circularity of the socioeconomic-water use linkage. That is, socioeconomic issues affect water use and conservation—and vice versa. Complicating the issue is the idea that socioeconomic understanding can be an important *intervening* step between water utility programs and the intended conservation effectiveness. We overcome this challenge using a conceptual model, presented in chapter 2, that distinguishes between socioeconomic impacts and characteristics and shows their relationships to utility conservation programs and customer conservation actions.

In the conceptual approach described in chapter 2, three relationships are considered. Each poses a question. First, how do socioeconomic characteristics of utility customers affect water use and conservation, independently of utility programs and activities? Second, what are the socioeconomic impacts of utility programs and activities (including pricing changes) on utility customers (especially their income)? Third, how do the socioeconomic characteristics of utility customers influence the effectiveness of utility programs and activities in achieving water savings and other goals?

This approach provides the framework for the review of issues and assessment tools. The study draws from previous analyses of these issues, as well as data and program information developed specifically for this report in collaboration with participating utilities. Case studies are used to illustrate a number of approaches that have been taken to address socioeconomic impacts. Utilities participating in this research as case-study partners include

- Los Angeles Department of Water and Power
- Phoenix Water Services Department
- City of Portland (Oregon) Bureau of Water Works
- St. Louis County Water Company

This report takes an empirical and descriptive approach, not a prescriptive one. No specific solutions are advocated to solve the difficult questions posed when considering the socioeconomic dimensions of conservation. Instead, a spectrum of information, analytic tools, and field experiences is provided so readers can judge for themselves what may be appropriate for their own communities and concerns.

WHY CONSIDER SOCIOECONOMIC ISSUES?

For the utility manager wondering why consideration of socioeconomic issues is important, six different and highly interrelated rationales can be provided. Many of these will be revisited throughout this report. Paying attention to socioeconomic considerations can help water utility managers

- Design effective conservation programs
- Achieve significant efficiency gains
- Reduce utility revenue losses
- Improve affordability for customers
- Enhance customer relationships
- Manage risk and uncertainty
- Respond to environmental justice concerns

Design Effective Conservation Programs

A reasonable assertion is that any utility program will be more effective in achieving goals if it recognizes and considers characteristics of the service population at large and the population expected to participate in the program. Methods that encourage participation by low-income customers, in particular, may require special attention on the part of the utility manager.

Socioeconomic traits can shape attitudes, which in turn can shape behavior. As noted in a study by Professors Durand and Allison,

> Knowledge of socioeconomic differences in conservation attitudes and actions is ... vital to the development of water management strategies. The adoption and successful implementation of any such strategy depends ultimately on public attitudes regarding conservation, upon the public's inclination to act upon such feelings, and upon the public's willingness to adopt specific measures. Moreover, knowledge of demographic differences

can help managers to target educational and other conservation programs as well as to identify areas of both policy conflict and consensus. (Durand and Allison 1995, 343)

By understanding the role of socioeconomic issues in water use and conservation, program designers can fine-tune their strategies for achieving program goals.

Achieve Efficiency Gains

Low-income housing conditions tend to provide opportunities for water conservation. For example, many low-income homes have older and less-efficient plumbing fixtures, as well as higher rates of leakage. Investment in conservation can yield water and monetary savings.

Water use by low-income households does not necessarily drive water system costs in the same way as water use by high-income households. A considerable amount of peak-period usage—an important capacity-cost driver—may be positively associated with the lifestyles of higher-income customers; examples are swimming pools and large landscapes. The potential water savings through conservation targeted to these uses can be substantial. Low-income households, by contrast, may account for a lesser share of total system demand, and savings from conservation (for example, from fixture repairs or replacements) may be associated with average or year-round usage. Nonetheless, the benefits of conservation can be highly relevant to the low-income service population because water savings are translated into financial savings, and even small improvements in affordability are meaningful.

When choosing among alternative conservation program measures and methods of implementation, the joint consideration of efficiency savings from the perspectives of both the utility and the customer is appropriate. Moreover, alternative conservation strategies can be evaluated in terms of joint implications for efficiency and equity and not merely confined to economic considerations.

Reduce Utility Revenue Losses

Rising water bills can burden customers, and when customers cannot afford to pay their water bills, utility finances suffer as well. Bad debt, write-offs, collection costs, and disconnection rates are indicators of payment difficulties. Individual water utilities often track trends in these areas.

Between 1990 and 1997, for example, the St. Louis County Water Company experienced a 50% increase in the value of utility write-offs (write-offs net of recovered amounts). Figure 1.1 provides a sample of some of the indicators used to monitor trends in disconnection actions and write-offs.

The impact of these losses on paying customers can vary substantially. Though some amount of revenue loss is expected in the course of utility business, these expenditures should not be considered "uncontrollable" when the utility might be able to address them through strategic programs. Targeted conservation programs, along with targeted assistance, can improve affordability and help reduce uncollectible accounts and revenue losses to the utility.

Improve Affordability for Customers

Water affordability will continue to be a serious problem for utilities and their customers. When low-income customers must pay more for water service, they must sacrifice other more

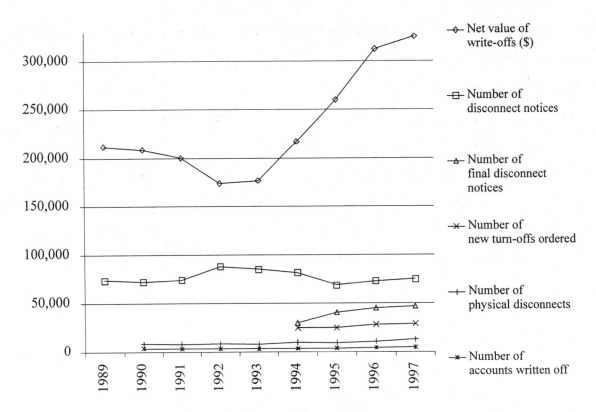

Source: Data provided by the St. Louis County Water Company.

Figure 1.1   Annual net value of write-offs for a sample water company: 1990 to 1998

discretionary goods and services (Rubin 1994, Bauman 1999, U.S. Department of Agriculture 1997, Edin and Lein 1997). As noted above, affordability problems can increase revenue losses to utilities; for customers, affordability problems jeopardize the quality of life.

Water conservation programs can help address affordability concerns. Well-designed programs not only reduce the tension between conservation and affordability but also help achieve these goals simultaneously. Reductions in water usage lessen the impact of rate increases. Some rate design and billing strategies can help address affordability issues directly while also helping accomplish conservation goals. Long-term efficiency accomplished through conservation will benefit utilities and their customers by helping to control capital and operating costs.

Program designers should know the distributional consequences of their plans. Programs can allocate benefits and burdens in various ways with various consequences. Programs that consider socioeconomic impacts can avoid or mitigate deleterious outcomes associated with some rate-design and program options.

Enhance Customer Relationships

Programs that recognize the diverse characteristics and needs of the service population are more responsive and will help build positive relationships in the community. Moreover, some evidence suggests that participating in utility programs improves bill payment by customers (Lent 1989). In an age of increasing competition, loyal customers may be the utility's most valuable assets.

Water utilities serve many types of customers in various situations. Customers are expected to be more responsive to programs that recognize their needs. Income is an important customer characteristic but certainly not the only one. Utilities should pay attention to other key socioeconomic indicators: household composition, housing, language and ethnicity, and special-needs populations. Language presents an excellent example. Utilities that serve Spanish-speaking service populations are well-advised to provide information on important issues, including water conservation and pricing, in Spanish. Utility personnel who speak Spanish also will be able to provide a more effective liaison to customers.

More generally, building strong customer relations requires the modern utility to be aware of the socioeconomic cleavages with its service population and to be sensitive about how these might affect or be affected by utility programs.

Manage Risk and Uncertainty

Managing uncertainty is one of the most important challenges that utilities face today. Utilities that acknowledge and plan for dealing with uncertainty are better positioned than those that do not (Chesnutt et al. 1995).

Programs that incorporate consideration of socioeconomic variables into financial planning will help the utility reduce uncertainty and achieve greater financial stability. The effects of conservation pricing and other programs can be modeled. Although the available assessment methods might not provide a high degree of precision, they can help inform the process.

A better practical and empirical understanding of how socioeconomic issues fit within the broader context of water use and utility programs can help managers recognize and plan for uncertainty. More informed and deliberative decision making, in turn, will lead to better program design and more predictable outcomes in the long run.

Respond to Environmental Justice Concerns

The differential impacts of public policies have long been a concern in the social sciences. The concept of environmental justice essentially captures the importance of considering how policies will have different effects on different subpopulations, understanding the potential for unfairness or inequity, and mitigating adverse impacts prior to their occurrence. Ignoring the implications of environmental injustice presents risks and thwarts policy implementation.

Modern policy and program design clearly should reflect the basic principles of social-impact analysis. With the signing of Executive Order 12898 by President Bill Clinton in 1994, consideration of environmental justice also became a matter of federal policy in the United States.* Pursuant to the order, federal agencies are required to develop an agency-wide environmental justice strategy to identify and address "disproportionately high and adverse human health or environmental effects of its programs, policies, or activities on minority populations and low-income populations." The agency strategy must endeavor to

---

* "Federal Actions To Address Environmental Justice In Minority Populations and Low-Income Populations," Executive Order 12898 (February 11, 1994).

- Promote enforcement of all health and environmental statutes in areas with minority populations and low-income populations
- Ensure greater public participation
- Improve research and data collection relating to the health of and environment of minority populations and low-income populations
- Identify differential patterns of consumption of natural resources among minority populations and low-income populations (Executive Order, February 11, 1994)

The President's order is not a mandate for water utilities—public or private—although it could affect interactions with federal agencies or programs. The underlying principles, however, offer a perspective worthy of consideration for enterprises in the service of a pluralistic public.

To round out why socioeconomic issues constitute an important consideration, let's look at a hypothetical town forum. We will call the location Diversetown, USA. This town is as diverse as America and as democratic as we all aspire to be. The town forum presented in Table 1.1 provides a flavor of the issues that conservation managers and customers face across this Great Land.

ORGANIZATION OF THE REPORT

This report is organized to provide water utility managers and policy makers with practical resources and tools for understanding and evaluating the socioeconomic issues associated with water conservation. The report includes the following:

- Chapter 2 provides the conceptual model for understanding the relationship of socioeconomic issues to water use and conservation and utility programs.
- Chapter 3 reviews the issues and findings related to the effects of socioeconomic variables on water use and water conservation.
- Chapter 4 examines the effect of water pricing and programs on socioeconomic conditions (especially income).
- Chapter 5 reviews water conservation programs that recognize the influence of socioeconomic factors.

Table 1.1

A town forum: Diversetown water utility's water conservation program

The Diversetown Water Utility held a town forum this evening to announce its new and comprehensive water conservation program. Utility officials presented the plan, which will consist of a year-round increasing-block rate structure, submetering of apartment buildings, a rate hike for commercial and industrial water use, a rebate program to encourage installation of efficient fixtures, a massive public education campaign, and a municipal grant to renovate golf course landscaping at the exclusive Diversetown Country Club. Officials said that, based on current water use patterns, the plan would result in significant water savings, and that the typical residential water bill would increase by only 7 percent.

Officials were somewhat surprised by the reaction of some of those attending the meeting:

Manny Mouths, a representative of the Coalition for Large Families, expressed concern about the increasing-block rate structure: "Larger families should not be penalized for water required for basic needs." He argued instead for a seasonal water rate that would place a greater price on summer water use above a basic threshold.

The seasonal proposal was immediately opposed by Harry Hamlet, of the Green Lawn Homeowners' Association, who argued that everyone in Diversetown benefited from the lush green lawns and that a seasonal rate might discourage beauty in the community. Gerry Attric, a member of the Diversetown Senior Garden Club and of the American Association of Retired Persons, added that seniors are on fixed budgets and should get a rate discount in the summer.

Florence Flats, who owns a number of Diverstown apartment buildings, praised the submetering proposal, saying that it will help renters understand that water use has a cost. She added that it also would improve her cash flow and increase her property value. Ralph Rentling, a student at the local community college, voiced an opposing view, arguing that renters should not pay directly for water because the landlord owns the building and should be responsible for seeing that the fixtures work and that leaks are repaired.

The Diversetown Chamber of Commerce expressed its concern that the hike in commercial and industrial rates might dampen economic development, jeopardize jobs, and possibly lead some industrial plants to seek an alternative water supply or shut down altogether. Sam Spotless, owner of the Spotless Car Wash Chain and President of the Chamber, added, "We are already doing what we can to save water—conservation is really an issue for residential customers." Teresa Tireless, who runs a homeless shelter on the west side of Diversetown, added that the higher rates would force a reduction in social services.

The rebate proposal was applauded as a way to encourage homeowners to replace older, less efficient toilets. Doug Dooright, a consumer advocate, voiced his concern that low-income customers would not be able to participate in the program because it would require an upfront cash payment that many west side customers could not afford. He also wondered whether the rebate could be used to retrofit fixtures designed especially for disabled residents of Diversetown.

Esther Esperanto, a teacher, expressed enthusiasm but also concern about the proposed public education program. Any program, she argued, must include materials responsive to the needs of Diversetown's many cultural and ethnic groups.

Renovation of the landscaping of the Country Club was perhaps the most controversial proposal. Club Director Dawn Fairway defended the proposal on the grounds that it would be the most cost-effective way to save water in Diversetown and that all residents would benefit. Mr. Spotless also stood in support of the plan. Ms. Tireless, Mr. Dooright, and Mrs. Esperanto rose in opposition, arguing that the plan would benefit Diversetown golfers at the expense of others.

The meeting was adjourned after the Diversetown Water Utility expressed its commitment to try to balance the need to conserve water with a consideration of the views expressed at the meeting.

- Chapter 6 provides a planning and evaluation framework, based on the conceptual approach, that water utilities can use for data collection and impact assessment.

- Chapter 7 reviews a number of specific analytical tools and provides illustrations of their use.

- Chapter 8 examines the socioeconomic impacts of water pricing, focusing on the income effects of rate changes and rate design.

- Chapter 9 discusses practical considerations for addressing socioeconomic considerations in program design and implementation.

Appendix A gives case-study background information, and the References provide a literature foundation for the report. We turn in chapter 2 to conceptual issues.

CHAPTER 2
BACKGROUND AND CONCEPTUAL APPROACH

BACKGROUND

How are socioeconomic factors relevant to the topic of water conservation? Is it that the socioeconomic characteristics of customers have an impact on how customers respond to conservation programs? If so, what is the role of socioeconomic characteristics in the design of utility water conservation programs? Is it that conservation programs have socioeconomic impacts on customers? If so, what is the role of program design in understanding and mitigating these impacts? Of course, all of these relationships are relevant. This chapter provides a conceptual framework for understanding the several ways in which socioeconomic factors relate to water conservation.

CONCEPTUAL MODEL

As indicated by the title of this report, this research exercise suggests a link between water conservation and socioeconomic impacts. Most conservation planners and analysts operate with their own understanding of the link between utility conservation programs and water use and conservation. This report emphasizes caution because there are many different ways to understand the link between programs and water use. Any single direct linkage neglects the potential importance of (1) socioeconomic characteristics as potential determinants of water use and conservation, independent of utility programs and activities; (2) socioeconomic impacts potentially caused by conservation programs; and (3) how socioeconomic characteristics of customers intervene to influence the link between utility conservation programs and customer water use and conservation.

A simplified conceptual model (Figure 2.1 and Table 2.1) is used here to illustrate how socioeconomic characteristics and socioeconomic impact variables are related to water use and conservation. In general, conceptual models such as the one presented here are used to organize concepts and formulate hypotheses. Models can help identify potential independent and dependent variables, as well as the relationships among them that form hypotheses about cause and effect.

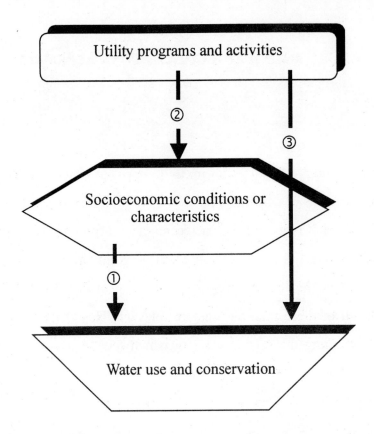

Figure 2.1 Conceptual model relating socioeconomic conditions and characteristics to water conservation

Table 2.1

Socioeconomic factors specified as variables

Relationship	Independent variable (cause)	Intervening variable	Dependent variable (effect)	Examples
①	Socioeconomic characteristics	—	Water use and conservation	Effect of key socioeconomic characteristics (income, housing, family size, ethnicity, and other factors) on water use and conservation.
②	Utility policies and programs	—	Socioeconomic conditions or characteristics	Effect of utility policies and programs (and inactions), including targeted and untargeted water conservation programs and pricing, on socioeconomic conditions (often defined primarily in terms of income).
③	Utility policies and programs	Socioeconomic conditions or characteristics	Water use and conservation	Effect of socioeconomics on conservation program outcomes, or the relationship between utility programs and water use and conservation behavior.

Independent (explanatory) variables represent potential causes; dependent variables represent effects; and intervening (interactive) variables shape or interact with the cause-and-effect relationship among other variables.

For the purposes of this report, a fully specified and integrated formal model is not attempted. No attempt is made to specify *all* the factors involved, the complete set of possible relationships, or the directions of hypothesized causation. At the risk of being reductive, this report presents a simplified view from the perspective of a water utility manager or planner responsible for water utility programs and activities, as depicted in Figure 2.1.

POTENTIALLY RELEVANT VARIABLES

Socioeconomic Characteristics and Impacts

As used throughout this report, *socioeconomic characteristics* refer to the demographic and related characteristics that might shape water use and conservation in significant ways. For example, a household's income and related characteristics affect that household's ability to pay for utility services, as well as qualifications for and dispositions toward participating in utility programs. Key socioeconomic characteristics may include

- Income
- Household composition
- Housing and property
- Language and ethnicity
- Special needs

Socioeconomic impacts refers to the effects of conservation programs related to income and, in particular, their "distributional" consequences. For the purposes of this study, socioeconomic variables (characteristics and impacts) can be organized into five general areas: income, household composition, housing and property, language and ethnicity, and special needs. Table 2.2 presents some selected socioeconomic characteristics of the U.S. population.

Table 2.2

Selected socioeconomic characteristics of the U.S. population

Income	
Median family income (1997)	$44,568
Persons below poverty level (1997)	35.6 million
Percent of persons below poverty level (1997)	13.3
Household composition	
Average size of household (1997)	2.64
Number of family households (1997)	70.2 million
Number of nonfamily households (1997)	30.8 million
Housing and property	
Percent owned (1997)	58.1%
Percent rented (1997)	30.3%
Percent vacant (1997)	11.6%
Median construction year as of 1995	1967
Median number of rooms (1995)	5.4
Median square footage (1995)	1,686
Ethnicity	
Percent White (1998)	82.6
Percent Black (1998)	12.7
Percent Hispanic (1998)	11.3
Percent Asian/Pacific Islander (1998)	3.8
Percent American Indian, Eskimo, Aleut (1998)	0.9

Source: U.S. Department of Commerce, 1999.

Income

Income, which tends to correlate with wealth, education, and property values, is an important determinant of water use. A positive relationship is expected between income and water use but not necessarily between income and water conservation. Often, income is considered jointly with price (which varies inversely or negatively with water use). Household income can play an important role in whether a customer has access to or participates in a program, such as a retrofit program. Programs that require participants to make even small investments can easily exclude low-income populations.

Income is the primary dependent variable when considering the socioeconomic impacts of water conservation programs. Changes in price and other programs that affect how much people pay for water service have an income effect.

Household Composition

The socioeconomic composition of households, including household size, can be an important determinant of water use. Indoor usage will vary with the number of people living in a household. Water habits also might vary according to the age of residents.

Housing and Property

Water use is likely to vary between single-family and multifamily properties. Owners of large properties are likely to consume more water for outdoor purposes (irrigation, car washing, and swimming pools). Outdoor usage plays an important role in driving peak demand and the costs that go along with meeting it.

Language and Ethnicity

Language and ethnicity are not known to play a highly significant role in terms of water use and conservation, although research in this area is limited. Language and ethnicity, however, may be important as intervening or interactive variables. There may be cultural barriers to participation in utility programs. Program effectiveness, in other words, may be affected by how the utility addresses cultural diversity in the service population.

Special-Needs Subpopulations

Finally, utilities serve special subpopulations. Even though all of these subpopulations might not play a significant role in overall water usage or conservation, the utility might want to guard against designing policies or programs that exclude or unduly harm specific groups. Senior citizens, for example, may have special concerns about accessibility and personal safety. Physically challenged consumers might be excluded from the benefits of a program if the program is designed exclusively with conventional practices or fixtures in mind. Special needs can arise in the context of residential water service, as well as commercial service for institutional facilities serving certain subpopulations (such as community centers and homeless shelters).

Water Use and Conservation

Water usage and water conservation either may affect or be affected by socioeconomic characteristics. Water use can be divided according to customer class, period of use (namely, season), and type of use (namely indoor versus outdoor).

Water conservation is defined as any beneficial reduction or modification of water use (Baumann, Boland, and Sims 1984). Conservation behavior may be induced in various ways through utility policies and programs. Price changes, for example, might indirectly provide incentives for customers to conserve water. Other programs provide various kinds of inducements.

Only during extreme conditions is water use regulated or restricted. Normally, customers are free to choose their level of investment in water usage or conservation, subject to the constraints of their income and other conditions.

Utility Policies and Programs

Conservation programs and programs implemented by utilities include but are not limited to the following examples:

- Retrofit programs for toilets or other devices
- Programs that provide rebates to customers
- Conservation activities that require customer expenditures
- Conservation-oriented rate structures
- Programs targeted to certain customer groups

Utility programs have the potential to affect all of their customers, including customers who do not directly participate.

RELATIONSHIPS AMONG VARIABLES

As noted in chapter 1, socioeconomic characteristics affect water use and conservation, and conservation programs can have socioeconomic impacts. Because a key variable such as income can be both an independent and a dependent variable, one must be careful in distinguishing which relationship is being discussed. These relationships are presented to illustrate several practical issues to utility managers.

How Socioeconomic Characteristics Affect Water Conservation

Relationship ①

The effect of socioeconomic characteristics on water use and conservation (non-use) can be expressed in the following functional form:

Water use and conservation = f_1 (socioeconomic characteristics of customers,
other variables)

Characteristics of individuals and groups can shape their consumption behavior, not only for water but also for other goods and services. A key determinant of consumer behavior, for example, is income. People at higher income levels consume more of many kinds of goods than people at lower income levels. The income elasticity of demand is a measure of how responsive demand is to changes in income.

Some socioeconomic characteristics may be more important than others in terms of influence on water consumption or water conservation, as well as the effectiveness of utility-sponsored conservation programs. Income obviously is a primary socioeconomic trait.

Income tends to correlate positively with water use because higher income levels correlate with lifestyles and spending patterns that include more water use (namely, big houses with more appliances and larger lots) (Baumann, Boland, and Hannemann 1998, especially chapter 2). As discussed later in this report, however, water demand may be price inelastic at lower income levels because a minimal quantity of water is a household necessity. In some areas, income in turn may correlate with the age and condition of housing (which plays a role in indoor usage) and residential lot size (which plays a role in outdoor usage).

Socioeconomic characteristics can affect whether and how households respond to utility conservation programs. For example, lower-income households may be less disposed to participate. If a program requires participants to make expenditures for fixtures, this may present a barrier to participation.

The implication is that utility managers should be aware that socioeconomic conditions in their service territory would affect their water conservation program efforts. In fact, socioeconomic considerations should be addressed explicitly in conservation program design and implementation.

Socioeconomic Impacts of Water Conservation

Relationship ②

The effect of water conservation programs on the socioeconomic condition of customers can be expressed in the following functional form:

Socioeconomic impact on customers = f_2 (utility policies and programs, other variables)

Socioeconomic impacts can be evaluated in terms of the distributional consequences of a change in policy or program, including water conservation efforts. A distributional effect occurs when an activity makes some group of customers better off or worse off at the expense or benefit of another group. The effects of policies can be measured and evaluated in terms of socioeconomic indicators, such as income. When evaluating socioeconomic impacts, attention to low-income households is especially important.

The actions—and inactions—of water utilities can affect water utility customers along a socioeconomic dimension, namely income. A cost-based increase in price to induce wise water use and conservation, for example, requires consumers to give up a greater share of their income if they continue to use the same amount of water. This is particularly apparent to customers who are not in a position to curtail their water usage.

Different conservation activities will have different distributional implications. For example, a conservation-oriented rate increase may have adverse distributional effects if water utility bills are regressive.[*] The same utility, however, also might introduce a conservation program targeted to the needs of low-income households. Thus, conservation programs can include activities that have mixed distributional effects.

The extent of the distributional effect depends in part on the nature of the program and the level of participation by different groups. If the cost of participating in a program is prohibitively high, the benefits of the program will be skewed toward those who can afford to participate. As discussed below, the variation in program participation rates also is one of the important ways in which socioeconomic circumstances affect conservation.

In the long term, to the extent that efficiencies are achieved, water conservation will be beneficial to society as a whole. The long-term distributional effects of conservation are indirect and less certain. Efficiency savings alone, however, provide no guarantee that all members of society will share equally or fairly in the benefits that efficiency provides.

Rate design choices—among classes, between fixed charges and variable rates, or between seasons—will have particularly salient income effects. Some customers will be more affected than others. To the extent that utility revenue requirements are treated as fixed in the short run, mitigation of these income (distributional) effects of programs can be viewed as a zero-sum game. Addressing an excessive income impact on one customer or set of customers requires that another customer or set of customers pay for it.

How Socioeconomic Characteristics Affect Conservation Program Effectiveness

Relationship ③

The effect of socioeconomics on the effectiveness of water utility conservation programs can be expressed in the following functional form:

Conservation program effectiveness = f_3 (water use, program participation)

---

[*] An expenditure (or a tax) is considered regressive if it takes a larger proportion of a lower-income household's budget than a higher-income household's budget.

The effectiveness of utility water conservation programs may depend, in part, on socioeconomic factors in the utility's environment. The intervening effect of socioeconomic characteristics occurs through current water use and through the decision by customers to participate in a conservation program. The identical program implemented in two communities with differing socioeconomic characteristics might produce radically different results. Water utilities can design and implement conservation programs that take locally relevant socioeconomic factors into account and thereby enhance program participation and improve overall effectiveness.

CAUSALITY AND ASSESSMENT

In this chapter we have presented a conceptual model and functional relationships that follow in terms of independent and dependent variables. We do not intend to imply that all of these relationships are causally defined or that this is the complete set of possible relationships. Rather, as a first step, we use the conceptual model to help identify useful questions. This, in turn, provides the foundation for later empirical analysis. Although this project does not include extensive empirical analysis, in the chapters that follow, we do provide descriptive evidence that helps us further define research questions and policy issues, and we provide an introduction to analytic assessment tools that can be used to answer these questions.

It is worth recounting the path that we have taken to arrive at the conceptual model presented in this chapter and that we use to structure this report. Socioeconomic impacts and characteristics are analyzed and considered in a number of social science disciplines, each of which brings with it its own insights and language—economics, political science, sociology, and management, to name a few. The empirical branches of these disciplines all rely on scientific methods composed of analytic models and empirical testing.

Our conceptual model is meant first and foremost to speak to the important issues that water conservation managers face, and secondarily to the research community. In fulfilling this aim, the conceptual model is designed to highlight practical issues and questions and to help communicate what are the important relationships. Certainly, many technical research issues, which are no less important to their respective audiences, are raised when applying each of the social science disciplines to our framework. Because our objective is not to produce a technical document for research, we make use of footnotes to address technical issues that are not targeted to our main audience.

Finally, the conceptual model provides the organization for the chapters that follow, with a chapter dedicated to each relationship:

- Chapter 3 reviews the issues and findings related to the influence of socioeconomic characteristics on water use and water conservation (Relationship ①).

- Chapter 4 examines the impact of water pricing and conservation programs on the socio-economic condition of customers in terms of household income (Relationship ②).

- Chapter 5 reviews water conservation and other programs that recognize the influence of socioeconomic factors on program design, participation rates, and results (Relationship ③).

CHAPTER 3
SOCIOECONOMIC CHARACTERISTICS AND WATER USE

INTRODUCTION

This chapter focuses on the first of the three relationships presented in chapter 2, the relationship between the socioeconomic characteristics of customers and their water use. How do socioeconomic characteristics of utility customers affect water use and water conservation, independent of utility programs?

To develop these concepts in the context of socioeconomic issues, conservation, and affordability, this chapter uses consumer expenditure data to illustrate, in a general sense, how water use varies between different service populations based on various socioeconomic characteristics. The chapter explores variations in water use according to income, household size, age, gender, region, ethnicity, employment, education, and other characteristics. The chapter also points out that consumer expenditures on water and other public services comprise a larger portion of income for low-income households than for high-income households.

The illustrations in this chapter draw on consumer expenditure data from the federal *Consumer Expenditure Survey 1997*, published by the Bureau of Labor Statistics (U.S. Department of Labor). This data source represents a wide range of socioeconomic variables that can be used to explore various characteristics. At the same time, the data have to be interpreted carefully because they are measures of consumer expenditures rather than water use.[*]

At the outset of our descriptive use of the consumer expenditure data, three important limitations should be noted:

1. Expenditures measure only the household budget burden and therefore serve as an imperfect proxy for household water use. Rates for water service are highly variable and the water bill has both fixed and variable (usage-based) components.
2. The expenditure category "water and other public services" in this database encompasses water, wastewater, and refuse-collection services.

---

[*] Economists note this distinction as the difference between the indirect (Hicksian) demand based on household expenditure minimization and the ordinary (Marshallian-Dupuit) demand based on observed consumption.

3. Expenditures are counted as "0" for households (including many renters) that do not directly pay for water and other public services. The effect is to understate these expenditures. Excluding the households that do not pay directly for water and other public services would result in higher mean values. Further, to the extent that more renters might be found in the lower-income categories (particularly in some geographic areas), the data do not reflect the indirect income effect of water bills paid through rents.

With these caveats in mind, this chapter explores how household expenditures for water seem to vary with some fundamental socioeconomic characteristics.

EXPENDITURES FOR WATER

For the typical household, water and other public services account for about 12 percent of the average household budget for utility services. Some real concern exists that rising costs will place considerable pressure on water bills and the budgets of lower-income households.

Aggregate consumer expenditure data provide some insight into the relationship between income and payments for utility services. Figure 3.1 shows how consumer expenditures on water and other public services vary across various demographic characteristics. Because these are simple descriptive statistics, we urge caution in drawing conclusions from this figure. For example, some of the demographic characteristics are highly correlated with income; we could speculate the professional degrees are not the reason for higher expenditures, but that these degrees yield higher income, allowing higher expenditures.

Income is an important determinant of expenditures for water. As incomes rise, expenditures for most categories of goods and services—including public utilities—also tend to rise. This does not imply that an increased paycheck directly causes increased water use. Instead, the relationship is one of association: Households having higher incomes tend to have more appliances to use, cars to wash, and landscapes to water. Indeed, as can be seen in Figure 3.2, consumer expenditures for water and other public services are higher for each income quintile. Households in the highest income quintile spend 2.75 times the amount spent by households in the lowest income quintile. As seen in Figure 3.3, this pattern holds for households of different sizes, although the

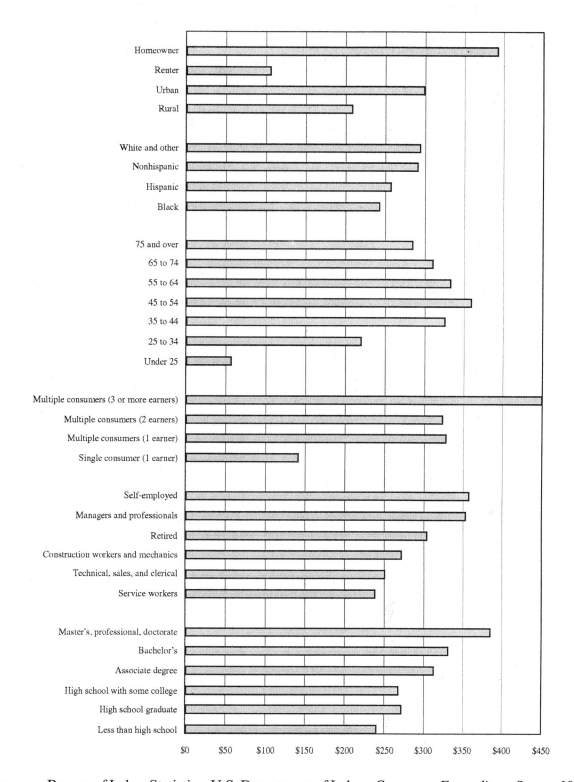

Source: Bureau of Labor Statistics, U.S. Department of Labor, *Consumer Expenditure Survey 1997.*

Figure 3.1   Annual consumer expenditures for water and other public services by demographic characteristics (1997)

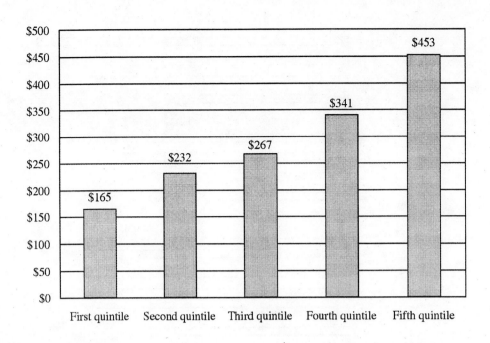

Source: Bureau of Labor Statistics, U.S. Department of Labor, *Consumer Expenditure Survey 1997.*

Figure 3.2   Average annual consumer expenditures for water and other public services by quintiles of income (1997)

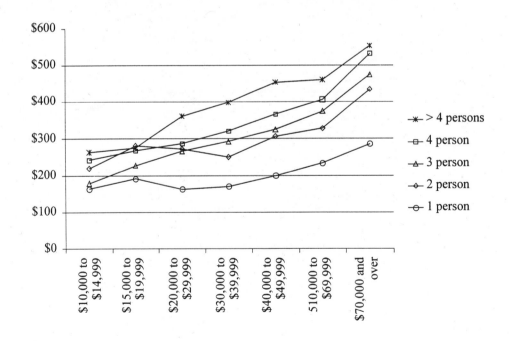

Source: Bureau of Labor Statistics, U.S. Department of Labor, *Consumer Expenditure Survey 1997.*

Figure 3.3   Average annual consumer expenditures for water and other public services by household size and before-tax income (1997)

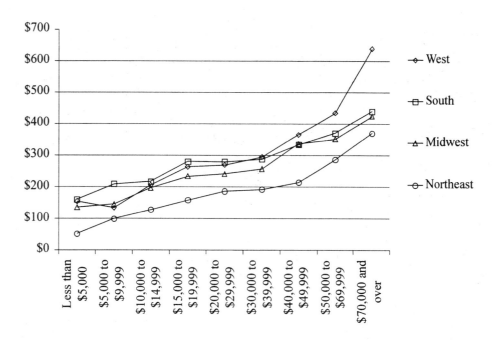

Source: Bureau of Labor Statistics, U.S. Department of Labor, *Consumer Expenditure Survey 1997.*

Figure 3.4   Average annual consumer expenditures for water and other public services by region and before-tax income (1997)

data also indicate—as expected—that households with more people also spend more for water and other public services.

These relationships can be viewed from various demographic perspectives. Figure 3.4 illustrates that expenditures for water and other public services are higher for higher income levels in each of the four geographic regions. Expenditures, however, are generally higher in the West and lower in the Northeast. Figure 3.5 shows that expenditures for water and other public services are higher for higher-income levels in each of several age categories. One theory posited for the apparently higher water use by high-income seniors is their interest in gardening. Figure 3.6 shows that consumer expenditures for water and other public services are higher for higher income levels for both single males and single females.

GROWTH, DECLINE, AND WATER USE

Aggregate water use patterns may be a provocative first step in detecting socioeconomic factors important to utility planning and conservation efforts. For illustration, we will compare

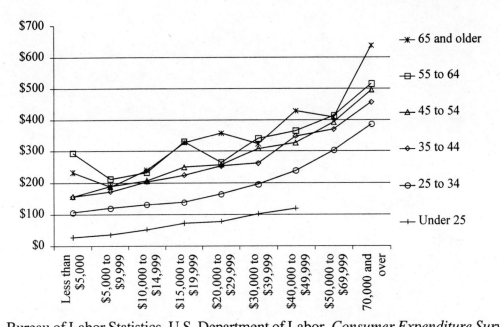

Source: Bureau of Labor Statistics, U.S. Department of Labor, *Consumer Expenditure Survey 1997.*

Figure 3.5   Average annual consumer expenditures for water and other public services by age and before-tax income (1997)

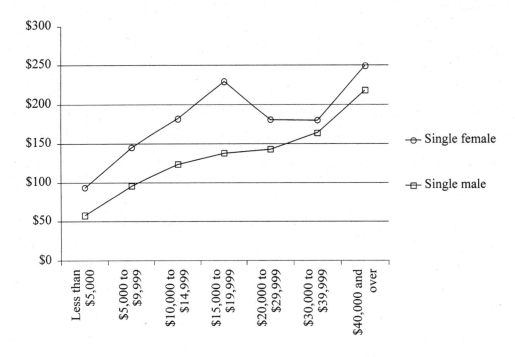

Source: Bureau of Labor Statistics, U.S. Department of Labor, *Consumer Expenditure Survey 1997.*

Figure 3.6   Average annual consumer expenditures for water and other public services by gender and before-tax income (1997)

two service territories in St. Louis County, Missouri, that began to experience major demographic shifts in the early 1980s. In this very general comparison, a growing and affluent (high-income) area is compared to a declining and poor (low-income) area. The results reveal patterns related to socioeconomic characteristics that are potentially important for water utilities.

In general, population growth is associated with growth in aggregate water use. This relationship is not always straightforward. For the declining area, Table 3.1 shows a comparable

Table 3.1

Comparison of socioeconomic characteristics and water delivered

for a growing and a declining service area (1990)

Variable	Growing area	Declining area
Socioeconomic Characteristic		
Population (1990)	9,510	3,612
Change in population from 1980	+6,335	−883
Percentage change in population from 1980	**+199.5%**	**−19.6%**
Persons per household (1980)	3.1	3.2
Persons per household (1990)	2.9	3.4
Percent minority or nonwhite (1990)	7.8%	93.1%
Median age (1990)	24.5	39.4
Median household income (1990)	$101,950	$12,300
Percent of persons below poverty line (1990)	1.8%	46.9%
Percent with college degree (1990)	55.9%	2.3%
Employment rate (1990)	98.2%	72.0%
Housing units (1990)	3,102	1,299
Change in housing units from 1980	+2,081	−252
Percentage change in housing units from 1980	+203.8%	−16.2%
Owner-occupied housing	85.6%	47.3%
Water Delivered		
Water delivered in 1980 (000)	254,531	600,797
Water delivered in 1990 (000)	1,035,548	457,452
Change in water delivered	+781,017	−143,345
Percentage change in water delivered (1980 to 1990)	**+307%**	**−24%**

Source: Demographic data are from the Missouri State Census Data Center (online). Water delivery data were provided by the St. Louis County Water Company.

reduction in population and water use (20 percent and 24 percent, respectively) between 1980 and 1990. The growth community, by contrast, has a 200 percent increase in population associated with a 300 percent increase in water deliveries. Ignoring the potential bias from the effect of climate over this time period, it can be surmised that the increase in water use is associated with population growth, new housing stock, and economic development.

Figure 3.7 shows trends in aggregate water use from 1970 through 1998 for the same two service areas. By 1998, residential customers accounted for about 60 percent of total metered sales in the growing area and about 53 percent of total metered sales in the declining area. The trend in water use *per connection* is provided in Figure 3.8.[*] The data reveal how water use increases with the growth in an affluent population and falls with population and economic decline. In other words, water-use patterns over time are closely connected with changing socio-economic conditions in the service territory.

The two communities also illustrate how water use varies seasonally in different service populations. Three years of quarterly billed residential water usage are provided in Figures 3.9 (aggregate) and 3.10 (per connection). The growth area shows substantially higher billings in August through October, which reflects summer usage (accounting for the lag caused by a quarterly billing cycle). In more affluent areas, seasonal variations in water usage can be substantial because of water use for landscaping. In lower-income areas, seasonal fluctuations may not be as great. In this illustration, a seasonal peak is not readily apparent for the declining area. Demand analysts may find it useful to evaluate temporal patterns of usage across areas that vary along income and other socioeconomic characteristics. Socioeconomic comparisons can be constrained by the available data. Even very general analyses, however, can provide managers with insights about potential socioeconomic impacts and design of water conservation programs.

WHY INCOME DRIVES WATER USE

Consumer expenditures for water and other public services increase with income, even when looking across a variety of socioeconomic characteristics at the same time, such as age, household size, geographic region, and gender. Income also is highly correlated with other

---

[*] Billing records alone, as used in this analysis, do not allow for a per-capita comparison.

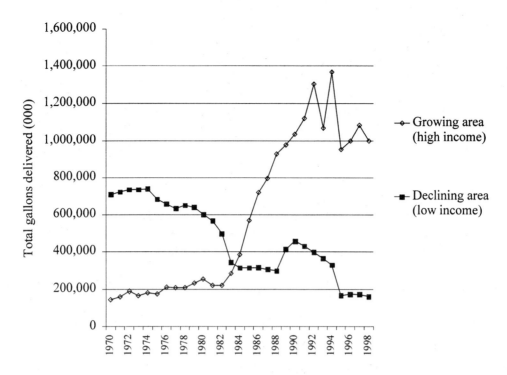

NOTE: All customer classes are included.

Source: Data provided by the St. Louis County Water Company.

Figure 3.7   Comparison of annual aggregate water use for two service territories

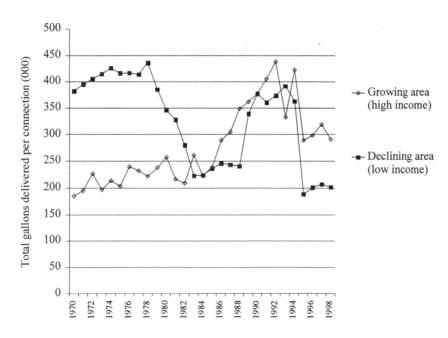

NOTE: All customer classes are included.

Source: Data provided by the St. Louis County Water Company.

Figure 3.8   Comparison of annual per-connection water use for two service territories

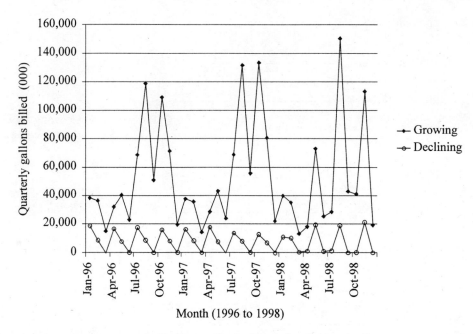

NOTE: The jagged pattern is a function of customer groups on different quarterly billing cycles.
Source: Data provided by the St. Louis County Water Company.

Figure 3.9   Comparison of quarterly billed aggregate water use for two service territories

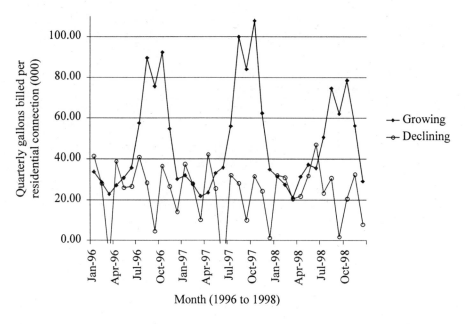

NOTE: The jagged pattern is a function of customer groups on different quarterly billing cycles.
Source: Data provided by the St. Louis County Water Company.

Figure 3.10   Comparison of quarterly billed per-connection water use for two service territories

socioeconomic indicators such as education, employment, housing characteristics, and life-styles. The relevance of income as a socioeconomic determinant of water use seems clear.

Why does income influence water use? The answer is that higher-income households have a higher propensity to use water-using appliances on site, such as dishwashers, clothes washers, swimming pools, and spas. Higher-income households often have more expansive and more intensely irrigated landscape areas. Car-washing and other more discretionary water uses are more prevalent. And, as discussed later, even relatively high water prices do not necessarily deter water usage by high-income households.

Not only do higher income households more often have water-using appliances (such as dishwashers and clothes washers), but usage levels for these appliances also seem to vary by income. A survey by the Energy Information Administration reveals a clear connection between income and hot-water usage by households, as illustrated in Figure 3.11.

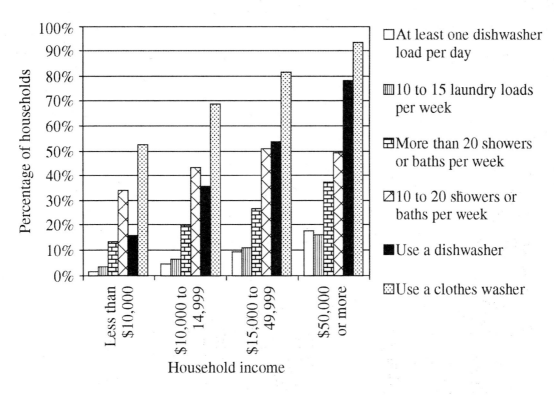

Source: Energy Information Administration, U.S. Department of Energy, *Residential Energy Consumption Survey*, 1997.

Figure 3.11   Household hot-water use by income (1997)

WATER DEMAND MODELING

Water demand modeling highlights the relevance and relative importance of socioeconomic characteristics in explaining water use. Water use is a function of a number of key variables, specifically

- Socioeconomic characteristics (including income)
- Climate and weather (temperature and rainfall)
- Price (average and marginal)

Socioeconomic characteristics are key determinants of water usage that are more completely understood within a broader analysis that also captures the effects of climate and prices.[*] This section focuses on the role of *income* in demand models. Although water utilities are limited in their ability to manipulate the climate or the prevailing socioeconomic conditions of their service territories, they can influence prices. This section considers socioeconomics as an input to water demand models; chapter 4 assesses the socioeconomic impacts of prices and price changes.

Key Variables

The prevailing models used to analyze and forecast water demand recognize the importance of socioeconomic indicators in explaining water use. These models measure the effects of both income and prices, along with other variables that affect water use. For example, the widely used IWR-MAIN model (developed by Planning and Management Consultants, Inc.) includes variables in three distinctive categories: socioeconomic characteristics (income, persons per household, and housing density), two price variables (marginal price and fixed charges), and two climate variables (maximum-daily temperature and total rainfall). Another important socioeconomic dimension is reflected in the separate estimations for single-family and multifamily water usage (which are further divided into summer and winter usage).

---

[*] Climate, weather, and other determinants of water use are important but tangential to the focus of this report. We refer readers to other sources for further information on these topics (for example, Baumann, Boland, and Hanemann 1998, and Chesnutt et al. 1996).

The default coefficients used in IWR-MAIN are reported in Table 3.2. These default values are based on a meta-analysis of nearly 200 estimates of residential water demand found in 60 empirical studies (Baumann, Boland, and Hanemann 1998, 100). The model suggests that income and persons per household are positively related to water usage. The coefficient for persons per household is slightly higher for winter usage. Housing density is negatively correlated with water usage, particularly for summer usage by single-family residences. The default assumptions in the IWR-MAIN recognize that weather has a strong influence on water usage. The model also clearly supports the relevance of income and other socioeconomic variables in affecting water usage.

The Role of Income

These findings suggest that changes in income are associated with changes in water use. Analysts often estimate *income elasticity of demand* to capture this effect in demand models. Income elasticity of demand usually is a positive coefficient, measured by the percentage change

Table 3.2

Coefficients used in IWR-MAIN demand model for water

Explanatory variable	Single-family		Multifamily/low-density	
	Summer	Winter	Summer	Winter
Socioeconomic variables				
Income	+0.40	+0.40	+0.40	+0.40
Persons per household	+0.40	+0.45	+0.40	+0.45
Housing density	−0.65	−0.30	−0.30	−0.15
Climate variables				
Maximum-daily temperature	+1.50	+0.45	+1.20	+0.35
Total rainfall	−0.25	−0.02	−0.10	−0.01
Price variables				
Marginal price	−0.25	−0.04	−0.15	−0.02
Fixed charge	−0.0005	−0.0005	−0.0005	−0.0005

Source: Planning and Management Consultants, Inc. as cited in Baumann, Boland, and Hanemann 1998, 100.

in demand divided by a corresponding percentage change in income. Except for "inferior goods," higher levels of income are expected to correlate with higher levels of consumption. Whereas the price elasticity of demand is represented by movements up and down the demand curve, the income elasticity of demand is represented by shifts in the demand curve (the price-quantity relationship) for different levels of income, as illustrated in Figure 3.12.

Income elasticity studies have been performed for various commodities, including water. A summary of findings is provided in Figure 3.13. Although water is responsive to changes in income, it not as responsive as many other consumer goods and services.

Water required for basic human needs—drinking, bathing, cleaning, and sanitation—probably varies little according to income (when controlling for household size and other factors). In fact, households with higher incomes might be more likely to have modern and more water-efficient fixtures, which could help lower per-capita consumption for some indoor uses. The positive relationship between income and water usage is anticipated primarily because of more discretionary water uses—both indoors and especially outdoors. Households with higher incomes are more likely to live in homes with larger lot sizes and higher irrigation needs. Households with higher incomes also might be more likely to use water for swimming pools, car-washing, and other purposes. A positive income elasticity coefficient thus can be hypothesized.

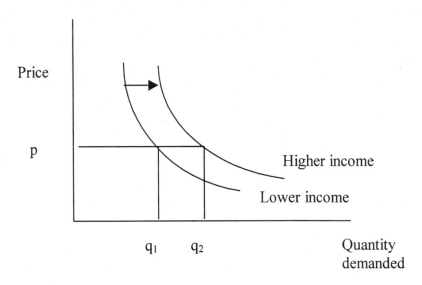

Figure 3.12   Demand curves for two income levels

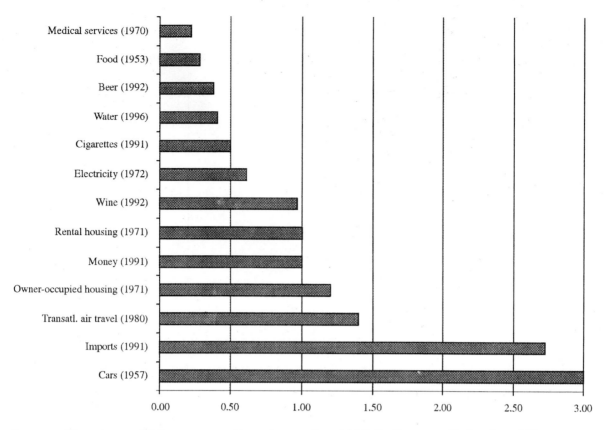

Source: Planning and Management Consultants, Inc. 1996 (in Bauman, Boland, and Hanemann 1998) for water estimate and Nicholson 1995 for all other estimates.

Figure 3.13   Comparative estimates of income elasticity of demand

Studies have found a range of income elasticities associated with water usage,[*] from less than .25 to more than 2.0 (summarized in Figure 3.14). Many estimates are within the .25 to .50 range, meaning that a difference in water usage of about 5 percent, a 10 percent difference in income, has been found to be associated with (Baumann, Boland, and Hanemann 1998). Other studies of various products have attempted to estimate differences in elasticities for ranges of income. For example, studies of food commodities have found that income elasticities are higher for

---

[*] Readers should note that the magnitude of estimated income elasticities does depend on what other drivers of demand are controlled for in the analysis. Analyses that include additional measures that are correlated with income (such as lot size, home size, and so forth) will estimate smaller income elasticity than analyses that use only income to explain this variation. Hence, the summary presented here should be taken as descriptive of published results; interpreting any one estimated elasticity requires knowledge of the other variables included in the analysis, data construction, and estimation method.

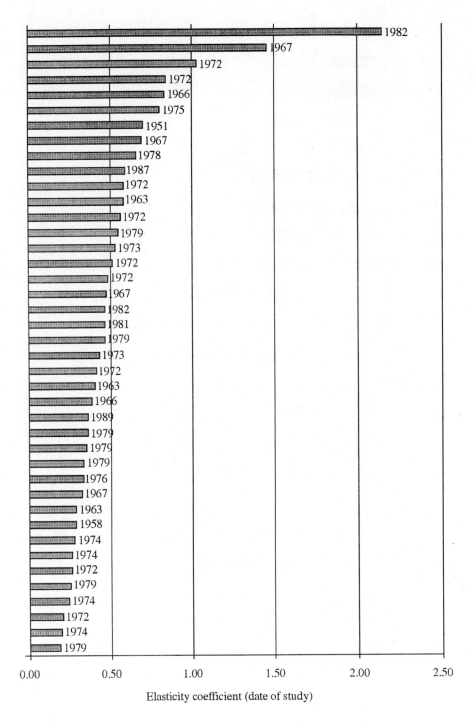

Elasticity coefficient (date of study)

Source: Adapted from Dziegielewski and Opitz (1991), in Baumann, Boland, and Hanemann 1998.

Figure 3.14 Estimates of income elasticity of water demand from selected studies

the lower-income groups (Park and Holcomb 1996). Purchasing by low-income households, thus, may be more sensitive to income variability.

SOCIOECONOMIC EFFECTS ON WATER CONSERVATION

Just as socioeconomic and demographic factors may affect water usage, they also may affect consumer views about conservation and actual conservation behavior. Understanding these relationships can help explain variations in conservation practices and facilitate program design.

As in water use, income is a potentially important variable in predicting conservation. Several studies have suggested that higher income is positively associated with conservation behavior. Downs and Freiden (1983) discovered that people with higher incomes and people with higher levels of education are more likely to engage in conserving behavior than people with lower incomes and those with lower levels of education. They also found that women are more likely than men to participate in conservation programs.

In another study, Sutherland (1994) found a statistical association between household income and participation in electric utility energy-conservation programs. Examining participation in utility rebates, energy audits, load-management programs, and other conservation measures, Sutherland discovered that high-income households are more likely to participate than low-income households in every case. The results of this study are summarized in Table 3.3.

Sutherland also suggests that participation in conservation programs is higher among people who live in newer residences and among people who already have undertaken significant conservation measures. Participants tend to have newer heating and cooling equipment and better-insulated homes than nonparticipants.

Sutherland's results suggest that the benefits of energy utility conservation programs disproportionately benefit high-income households, while low-income households, which spend a higher proportion of their income on energy, receive few benefits. Furthermore, because those who participate most in the energy conservation programs already are performing energy-efficiency measures, the payoff in potential energy savings is relatively low. Many of the high-income households, then, are "free riders." Although low-income households have the greatest opportunity to achieve significant savings, they benefit least from the conservation programs studied. According to Sutherland

41

Table 3.3

Participation in energy conservation programs by income class

| | Participation rates | | | | |
Income class	Any program	Rebate	Load control	Energy audit	Other
Less than $5,000	1.05	0.34	0.71	0.00	0.00
$5,000 to $9,999	1.95	0.76	0.00	0.73	0.70
$10,000 to $14,999	5.68	1.24	0.55	1.98	1.91
$15,000 to $24,999	5.85	1.23	2.79	1.66	1.67
$25,000 to $34,999	5.40	1.97	0.84	1.62	1.41
$35,000 to $49,999	5.70	1.38	1.37	0.79	1.31
$50,000 or more	8.84	2.21	4.76	1.84	2.57
Average	5.79	1.49	2.29	1.41	1.61

Source: Sutherland 1994.

(1994), "One implication is that utility conservation programs are redistributing wealth from low to high income households."

In another study, Allen and Davis (1993) discovered somewhat different results. In an examination of coupon incentives to promote aluminum recycling, they found that income, gender, and occupation are most associated with recycling behavior. Unlike other studies associating high income with conservation behavior, Allen and Davis found that nonprofessional males with low incomes are most likely to participate in the aluminum recycling programs. They also discovered that these recyclers actually are "slightly cynical of the positive ecological consequences of recycling."

The motivating factor in this program seemed to be the economic incentive to recycle, suggesting that economic incentives might be an important factor in getting low-income households to participate in conservation programs. According to Allen and Davis, people who did not consider themselves recyclers did not participate as much in the coupon incentive program as those who always were recyclers. Similar to Sutherland's finding that households with existing energy conservation practices tended to participate more in the utilities' conservation programs, Allen and Davis concluded that the coupon incentive program encouraged current recyclers to recycle even more.

A study of households in Houston, Texas, by Durand and Allison (1995) also revealed a tendency for low-income households to conserve water more than high-income households. This survey indicates that people with higher household incomes and with higher educational levels rate water savings as less important to them personally. Furthermore, lower-income households seemed more likely than higher income households to reduce interior residential water use. The researchers also discovered that larger households were more likely than smaller households to repair leaks and plumbing problems.

Although drawing conclusions from the few available empirical studies is difficult, a few points can be noted

- Water conservation behavior may vary with socioeconomic characteristics just as water usage does.
- Faulty program design can lead to free ridership and a distributional effect that favors high-income households at the expense of low-income households.
- Appropriate incentives are needed to encourage participation on the part of households that will benefit most from conservation in terms of water and monetary savings.

OBSERVATIONS

These findings illustrate that water usage is connected to socioeconomic characteristics. In particular, households with higher incomes are expected to spend more on water, along with other public utility services. It makes sense for water managers to try to understand how these relationships may be relevant in their own service territories. Often, these analyses can be performed using data that are readily available from water-system billing systems.

If all other things are equal, higher-income households are expected to use more water for two reasons: (1) their ownership of water-using assets is higher and (2) their usage may be higher as a result of lifestyle factors. Because of their higher water use, high-income households can have ample opportunities for water savings from conservation programs. Lower-income households often have fewer water-using appliances and use less water overall, which might constrain conservation opportunities to some extent. Exceptions to this rule include differences in socioeconomic characteristics such as the age of housing and number of persons living in the household who affect the potential for savings. For individual households, however, the water savings might not be as meaningful as the cost savings associated with water-use reductions. Thus, improving service affordability can be an ancillary goal, if not a primary goal, for water conservation programs targeted to low-income households.

Understanding the socioeconomic dimension of water use will help managers understand how changes in demographics might change patterns of water demand. This has obvious importance for demand forecasting. As discussed in subsequent chapters, it also provides a backdrop for understanding how socioeconomic factors also influence water conservation pricing and programs.

CHAPTER 4

SOCIOECONOMIC IMPACTS OF PRICING AND PROGRAMS

INTRODUCTION

As already introduced, water utility policies and programs can have significant socioeconomic impacts. The decisions—and nondecisions—that utilities make have distributional consequences for the populations they serve. That is, utility actions can make the condition of customers (or certain groups of customers) better or worse at the expense or benefit of other customers. Water pricing has direct distributional consequences because rate levels determine how much households pay for water service and because rate design decisions determine how costs are allocated among customers, or "who pays." Conservation programs allocate costs and confer benefits, too. Although the distributional effects of programs might seem less direct than the effects of pricing, they are no less meaningful.

When assessing the socioeconomic impact of utility programs, income is a primary consideration. Though other metrics might be used, income is an essential indicator of socioeconomic condition. The distributional consequences of pricing and other conservation programs can be readily understood in terms of income. Higher water bills take a higher share of household income, leaving less available to purchase other goods and services, or to save. Similarly, high program-participation costs take a share of income and can offset the benefits of water savings through conservation.

This chapter focuses on the socioeconomic impact of water pricing because price plays a central role in promoting efficiency and conservation. Subsequent chapters provide some evaluation tools for assessing the impacts of price changes.

PRICE IMPACTS

Distributional Effects of Prices

All other things constant, as discussed in chapter 3, water use generally rises with income. At higher income levels, households spend more on water as well as other utility services. But the distributional impact of water bills is not uniform across income groups. Although higher-income households spend more on water and public services in absolute dollars, they spend less on utility services in proportion to their total income and expenditures.

Figure 4.1 illustrates the relationship between household income and expenditures for utilities, including expenditures for water and other public services. The data reveal that low-income households devote a much higher percentage of resources to utility services (a regressive effect). Affordability of utility services obviously is an issue for many low-income households. At higher income levels, the percentage of income paid for utilities (and the percentage of total consumer expenditures paid for utilities) declines.

This general pattern holds for water and other public services, which include wastewater and solid waste charges, although the differences are not dramatic. Indeed, compared to overall expenditures, water and other public services take a fairly steady share of expenditures across income groups.

The relative proportion of income and expenditures devoted to water and other public services seems to decline for the lowest income categories before stabilizing. The data, however,

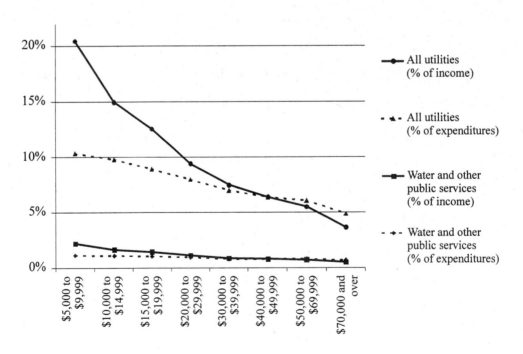

Source: Bureau of Labor Statistics, U.S. Department of Labor, *Consumer Expenditure Survey 1997.*

Figure 4.1   Utilities as percentage of after-tax income and expenditures (1997)

understate both absolute and relative expenditures because households that do not directly pay for these services ("0" expenditures) are included in the averages.[*]

The generally regressive nature of utility services is relevant for utility planners and analysts. Changes in prices will be more consequential for lower-income customers. Water conservation and assistance programs also should consider the cost of participation, which can present a barrier for low-income households. Finally, utilities can design programs that explicitly address or mitigate adverse distributional consequences of pricing and other programs.

Pricing as a Conservation Tool

Water metering and pricing are fundamental tools of water management and conservation. To achieve economic efficiency, water prices should reflect the marginal cost of water. The price signal encourages efficient consumption on the part of consumers and efficient production on the part of producers.

Pricing is so vital to conservation that an efficiency-oriented rate is considered a necessary, albeit not always sufficient, component of a conservation program or strategy. Conservation pricing often is combined with public education and other programs. Efficiency-oriented pricing emphasizes metering and the variable component of the water bill. A metered rate produces a water bill that varies with the amount of water used. Higher use results in a higher bill, and lower use results in a lower bill. From an efficiency standpoint, the metered rate should reflect the economic value of water service.

But higher water bills are less affordable to households that have lower incomes. Furthermore, lower-income households may have less ability to reduce water demand because of higher household density, lack of capital for water-efficiency devices, and less consumption for landscape irrigation. In other words, efficiency-oriented pricing can have adverse socioeconomic impacts. To effectively address both policy goals, utility companies must address the potential tension between conservation and affordability.

---

* See the important caveats on the use of consumer expenditure data in chapter 3.

Prices and Income

The effect of a change in price has two parts: the "substitution effect" and the "income effect." The substitution effect of a price change is the change stemming purely from the price change. For example, if the price of water goes up relative to other goods, most consumers would buy less water and more of other goods. The income effect recognizes that when the price of one good goes up, say the price of water, consumers have less buying power. It is as if consumers have less income, and therefore is called the "income effect." The total change in water use induced by a change in price is the sum of the price and income effects.[*]

As discussed in chapter 3, a positive relationship exists between income and water use, measured as income elasticity. Price elasticity, on the other hand, measures changes in the quantity demanded as associated with changes in the price for the good or service. The price elasticity of demand is a negative number. Based on a price elasticity of –0.2, for example, a 10 percent increase in price is associated with a 2 percent decrease in usage.

The price elasticity for water demand has been estimated in a variety of empirical studies (Beecher et al. 1994). The same models used to estimate income elasticity are used to estimate price elasticity. These studies are imperfect to the extent that they use aggregate data to test microeconomic theory about individual responses to changes in price, which will likely vary among disaggregated subgroups. Most of these studies are confined to a single time period (cross-sectional); few studies actually examine changes in price and quantity for a group of customers over time.

Figure 4.2 shows elasticity estimates for a diverse range of consumer items. Water seems to be less responsive to changes in price than do other consumer goods and services. Studies generally have found that, in the short term, residential water demand is relatively price inelastic (Table 4.1).[†]

---

[*] In formal terms, this relationship is affectionately known as the Slutsky equation. A price change translates into demand change by two effects: the substitution effect and the income effect. The first price effect may be the one most familiar to readers; if something becomes more expensive, we consume less of it. The second price effect suggests that a price increase also reduces our income; this can change our consumption, too.

[†] Nonresidential (commercial and industrial) water consumption is considered more responsive to changes in price. The price elasticity of demand for the nonresidential sector has been estimated to range from –50 to –80 (Dziegielewski and Opitz 1991).

48

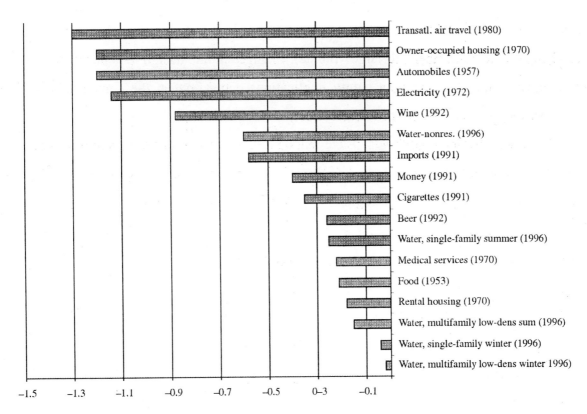

Source: Adapted from Planning and Management Consultants, Inc. 1996 (in Baumann, Boland, and Hanemann 1998) for water estimates, and Nicholson 1995 for all other estimates.

Figure 4.2   Comparative estimates of price elasticity of demand for water and other goods and services

Table 4.1
Estimated short-run price elasticity of demand for water

	Winter usage	Summer usage
Single-family residential customers	−.00 to −.10	−.10 to −.20
Multiple-family residential customers	−.00 to −.05	−.05 to −.10

Source: Chesnutt et al. 1996.

These estimates support the idea that winter (or indoor) water use is inelastic (or unresponsive to changes in price). Summer (or outdoor) use is also inelastic but somewhat more price-responsive. Water use by multifamily residential customers also is less responsive to price than water use by single-family customers. If multifamily housing tends to consist of lower-income customers, this finding has implications for affordability. Price changes will not induce significant reductions in use that could lower total water bills. Residential water use also is less responsive to price changes than nonresidential (large-volume). Changes in rate design to achieve conservation and other goals may have varying equity implications depending on the demographics of the service territory and the features of the rate structure.

For lower-income households, usage will be less responsive to changes in price because a greater proportion of use is likely to be less discretionary and less price-responsive. Furthermore, poor households may not have the capital necessary for installing and maintaining conservation devices. Renters, in particular, may not be permitted to change plumbing fixtures or make other improvements. Water use by renters usually is unmetered, so pricing will be a less effective conservation tool. Thus, price increases imposed on renters—whether through direct billing to the household or indirectly through rents—can place a hardship on households. Renters also may feel the effect of commercial rate increases, such as the cost of using common apartment or neighborhood laundry facilities.

Pricing also may be relatively ineffective for higher-income customers because affordability is not an issue. Higher-income households have more discretionary water use, including outdoor use. But reductions in demand as a result of price increases can be offset by increasing income.

Research Findings

A 1993 study, noting the relative inelasticity of water demand for apartment dwellers, articulates some of the potential implications for pricing policy,

> These findings suggest a dilemma in the pricing of water services. Because the income elasticity of demand is relatively low, economic growth does not bring large revenue growth for the water system. Furthermore, because the elasticity of demand with respect to marginal price is relatively low, the supplier has an incentive to increase the marginal price as revenue needs increase. This trend leads to increased cutoffs of low-income households, which not only leads to substandard living conditions but also raises public health concerns. Water and sewer service therefore has some characteristics of a public good, in the sense that if my neighbor's service is cut off, both of us suffer.

50

The design of rates for water service should take these public goods considerations into account. On the one hand, marginal price should be high enough for upper levels of consumption so that overuse and waste is discouraged. On the other hand, the average price for basic consumption levels should be low for low-income households.... Innovative pricing schemes, which balance the efficiency goals calling for marginal cost pricing with the equity and public goods goals calling for cutoff avoidance, should be the order of business in the design of water service rates. (Whitcomb, Yingling, and Winer 1993)

Martin and Wilder (1992) estimated the price elasticity of residential demand for water services, while also examining payment delinquency. Demand was estimated using both average and marginal price (the latter of which is a less robust determinant). Income effects were statistically significant but small, ranging from .04 to .27. Delinquency rates were inversely related to income and positively related to price; the burden of increased rates includes service termination. The authors found that monthly cutoff rates can be as high as 5 to 7 percent of the total customer base.

CONSERVATION AND AFFORDABILITY

Table 4.2 provides a basic framework for understanding the connection between conservation and affordability. The framework represents the following functional relationships:

➜ Affordability = f (water bill and ability to pay)
   ➜ Ability to pay = f (socioeconomic conditions and income assistance)
      ➜ Water bill = f (water rate and water usage)
         ➜ Water rate = f (cost of water service and rate structure)
            ➜ Rate structure = f (cost allocation, rate design, and billing structure)
               ➜ Cost of water service = f (capital costs and operating costs)

These relationships point to some of the specific ways by which the affordability of water service can be addressed. Obviously, keeping costs lower helps keep prices lower for everyone. One of the goals of strategic conservation is cost reduction. More immediately, conservation that helps reduce usage can lower bills. Affordability also is affected by methods of allocating costs and designing rates. As discussed in the next section, some rate structures are perceived as more affordable than others.

Table 4.2

Framework for understanding conservation and affordability

Affordability							
Customer's ability to pay		Customer's water bill				Costs of water service	
			Water rate				
			Rate structure				
Socioeconomic conditions	Income or payment assistance	End-use water usage	Cost allocation	Rate design	Billing cycle	Capital costs	Operating costs
Affects ability to pay. Conservation cannot directly alleviate socioeconomic conditions (e.g., lack of jobs or low incomes). However, more efficient use of societal resources will positively affect the economy.	Utilities can help facilitate the creation of and participation in income or payment assistance programs for customers in need (e.g., grants, vouchers, voluntary contributions).	Demand management measures can help customers reduce water usage and lower total water bills. Conservation programs can be targeted to the needs of low-income customers.	Allocation among classes of customers and among customers within classes (e.g., peak vs. off-peak users) affects the rate to residential users.	Several rate design techniques can be used to maintain a lower rate for basic (essential) usage. Lifeline rates can be designed to achieve both conservation and affordability goals.	More frequent billing sends a clearer rate signal and can improve affordability for some customers.	Some infrastructure costs can be avoided, postponed, or reduced through conservation and efficiency improvements, which in turn help keep rates lower.	Some operating costs can be reduced through conservation and efficiency improvements, which in turn help keep rates lower.

IMPLICATIONS FOR PRICING POLICY

Lifelines and Discounts

A lifeline rate provides a block of water service, designed roughly to meet basic needs, at an affordable rate. Lifeline rates do require subsidies from other customers (residential, nonresidential, or both). The rate also can be designed as an increasing-block or seasonal rate, which can serve to intensify the conservation-orientation of the price signal. Lifeline rates share some traits with other conservation-oriented rates (such as seasonal rates, excess-use rates, or indoor-outdoor rates) based on generally marginal-cost pricing principles (Beecher 1994). The first block of usage, priced at a rate below marginal cost, can be justified as an amount considered essential and necessary for human health. Additional usage, priced at higher rates, then would be for other uses.

Assuming that some amount of safe, potable water does provide a benefit to society, in terms of improved public health, one can reconcile lifeline rates with social efficiency. Using the concept of social accounting prices, Albouy (1997) developed an economic framework to incorporate the social benefit of universal service provision of potable water: "This theoretical framework provides a justification for life-line rates well under marginal cost in the case of consumption with a [high] social value... ." (Albouy 1997, 23). Thus, it is possible for utilities to use the rate structure to achieve multiple policy goals, such as improved affordability and conservation.

Figure 4.3 illustrates the basic idea of combining lifeline and a greater degree of conservation pricing. Customers who can maintain their water usage at a moderately low level will benefit from lifeline rates. Obviously, these rates help keep water bills affordable for basic needs. This, in turn, reduces the requirement for disconnection and its associated costs. Reducing the utility's bad debt and collection costs benefits the utility and all of its ratepayers (who ultimately must pick up these costs). Thus, lifeline rates can play an important role in providing safe, potable water to all—that is, the concept of universal service.

General lifeline rates can be easier to administer than rates requiring eligibility. A drawback of a generally available lifeline rate is that it is not targeted only to needy customers. Some customers with the ability to pay for service will benefit (the "free-rider" problem). Many utilities object to implementing lifeline rates. In general, utilities can be reluctant to take on what they

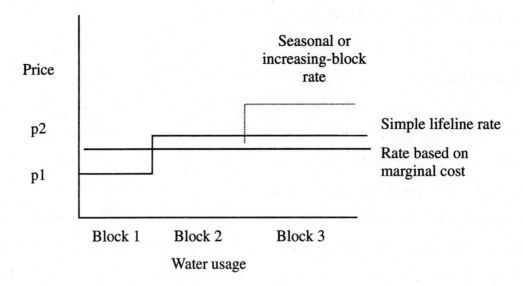

Figure 4.3   Illustration of lifeline rates

consider to be a societal problem. Utilities are especially opposed to using the rate structure for this purpose. The technical reason often cited is that these rate structures violate traditional cost-of-service principles and add to revenue instability:

> Rate structures designed to meet conservation objectives often have the added benefit of holding down costs for customers with very small usages, the group most often singled out as the focus of "affordable" water.... Conservation rates, low customer charges, elderly/low-income discounts, and other measures are implemented in hope of improving the "affordability" of water. Unfortunately, these measures force the utilities to experience much more variability in revenues with changes in consumption, either due to increased customer conservation or due to weather conditions. These revenue fluctuations can result in affordability problems for the utility itself. (Day 1993, 3)

Nevertheless, a well-designed rate that properly determines the lowest usage block based on minimum essential use, combined with eligibility criteria that make customer participation predictable, may not result in substantial revenue problems. According to AWWA Manual M34, "Lifeline rates and low-income discounts do not present a major obstacle to revenue stability, though they may be less stable than some other rate alternatives" (AWWA 1992, 12). Moreover, it has been argued that, under some circumstances, conservation-oriented rates can enhance revenue stability by shaving peak demands (Amatetti 1994, 184).

Some state legislatures may force consideration of lifeline rates or other pricing mechanisms to address the affordability problem. Massachusetts enacted, but later repealed, a statute requiring communities receiving state revolving loan funds to adopt a pricing structure that "provides for assurance of service to households who by reason of low income are unable to pay the charge for service."* The act also required state officials to examine possible extension of benefits to renters. Rising water costs and prices may lead state legislatures to seek other means of encouraging communities to consider affordability policies. State public utility commission experience with lifeline rates for water utilities is limited.

Metering and Billing

Some forms of relief involve changes that utilities can implement to make customer bills somewhat more manageable, if not substantially more affordable (Beecher 1994). Many water utilities bill their residential customers quarterly; some use even longer billing cycles. Although it can save utilities administrative costs, quarterly billing has several drawbacks compared to monthly billing. With quarterly billing, the price signal to customers may be too infrequent to influence consumption behavior in a timely way. For example, a customer may use water for landscaping all summer long and not realize the water-bill consequence until autumn. Another drawback to quarterly billing is that rate-design choices are constrained. The effectiveness of a seasonal or excess-use rate to encourage reductions in peak demand, for example, depends on monthly billing. Finally, from an affordability standpoint, quarterly billing is a problem because customers with low or fixed incomes are confronted with a large bill every three months rather than a supposedly more manageable bill every month. Changing the billing cycle, however, may not be beneficial for customers in buildings where master metering for water service is used and costs are passed along to consumers through rents.

Budget billing is a specific form of monthly billing (offered by many energy utilities) that spreads costs evenly across the 12 months to mitigate the effects of high bills from high seasonal use (such as winter heating). Seasonal peaks also occur for residential water demand. Much (but not

---

* Chapter 275 of the Massachusetts Acts of 1989, Section 15, as cited in Saunders et al. 1998.

55

all) of the higher summer demand can be attributed to increased outdoor water use (landscaping, swimming pools, and car-washing), and many of these activities are associated with higher-income populations. Somewhat less seasonality in low-income populations may limit the usefulness of budget billing in terms of improving manageability and affordability. The chief drawback of budget billing is that it mutes price signals. Nonetheless, budget billing can be explored as an option for addressing affordability concerns.

For some water utilities, monthly billing may provide a method to reduce rate shock to customers in the face of rising costs and prices. In a 1994 survey, public utility commission staff members in Massachusetts, New York, and Vermont reported that billing cycles were changed for some jurisdictional water utilities for the purpose of mitigating rate shock to customers (Beecher 1994). Another form of assistance is to adjust actual billing dates so bill payment can be coordinated with a customer's receipt of public-assistance benefits.

Of course, changing the billing cycle does not address the actual cost of water, only how it is recovered from customers. Monthly billing might enhance the utility's revenue stream. Stepping up the meter-reading and billing cycle, however, also can add substantially to a utility's administrative costs (including personnel, processing, printing, and postage costs). Smaller water systems may lack the resources to implement monthly billing. The potential costs and benefits of billing-cycle changes must be carefully assessed by utilities and regulators prior to implementation.

Submetering

The issue of submetering provides an excellent example of the potential tension between efficiency and equity goals. Submetering is used to separately meter and bill customers within multiunit apartment buildings, condominiums, and mobile home parks.

As a generalization, metering is essential for efficiency-oriented pricing. Efficient prices are calibrated to usage, sending customers an appropriate signal about the value of water. Submetering might be viewed as a logical extension of metering, and therefore an appropriate component of a conservation program. Submetering can be an effective tool of conservation under certain circumstances. Under other circumstances, submetering can be ineffective and can inflict adverse socioeconomic impacts.

Submetering may be ineffective or harmful for several reasons. First, the effectiveness of submetering depends on the degree of price-responsive water use on the user's premises. As already noted, indoor use also is less price-responsive and therefore less price elastic, so the effect of a price signal on consumption decisions is weak.[*]

A second consideration is the ownership of water-using fixtures and appliances. The price signal cannot induce customers to repair leaks or replace equipment they do not own. Apartment dwellers do not own plumbing equipment and typically do not own appliances. Of course, many apartments are not equipped with some kinds of water-using appliances, such as clothes washers and dishwashers. More transient populations also have little incentive to make repairs or purchases that will not provide a benefit if they move. Condominium owners, however, might be more responsive to price signals in this regard.

A third consideration is that shifting the bill to customers actually removes the incentive for landlords to invest in efficiency. In effect, the price signal is taken away from the party who can respond and is redirected toward a party who cannot respond. A related problem is the loss of economies of scale and scope that landlords can use to their advantage in renovating an entire building (as compared to a single unit).

In sum, the introduction of metering and especially submetering raises significant socio-economic concerns. Moreover, as summarized in Table 4.3, metering and submetering introduce incentives that may be more effective in meeting some conservation goals than others.

Summary of Pricing Impacts

Table 4.4 provides a summary of the conservation and socioeconomic impacts associated with some basic metering, pricing, and billing strategies. The key message for water managers is that anticipating these impacts is important to designing rate structures that are effective in meeting goals. In some cases, it may be necessary to resolve tradeoffs between conservation goals and socioeconomic impacts.

---

[*] Apartment dwellers tend to have less discretionary water use; mobile home tenants might have some outdoor usage. Water can be used for irrigation of common grounds in apartment complexes, in which case the landlord is billed.

Table 4.3

Effectiveness of metering practices in achieving metering goals

| | Metering goal | |
Method	Improve efficiency of water-use fixtures	Improve efficiency of water-use behavior
Metering	High Induces landlords/owners with price-elastic usage to make efficiency improvements, including repairs and replacements; tenants may not realize benefits in terms of lower rents.	Moderate Induces landlords/owners to implement outdoor efficiency practices, as well as to provide information to tenants regarding indoor efficiency practices; however, owners are dependent on tenants to change indoor-use behavior and tenants may not realize benefits in terms of lower rents.
Submetering	Low Shifts incentives away from landlords/owners and toward tenants, who are less likely to make capital investments in plumbing improvements and efficient fixtures because of ownership, affordability, and transience.	Moderate Shifts costs and may induce tenants to adopt water efficiency behavior; however, relatively low price-responsiveness for indoor usage may limit water savings.

MITIGATING RATE IMPACTS ON POOR HOUSEHOLDS

A project of the AWWA Research Foundation (AWWARF) addresses the need for water utilities to address the potential gap between water prices and the ability of low-income households to pay for water service (Saunders et al. 1998). The report also provides a bill-analysis method that specifically addresses rate impacts on very low-income households.

The report focuses on water rates and rate structures that help keep the total water bill to an affordable level. For water service, an affordability threshold of 2 percent of household income is used; for water and wastewater services combined, a threshold of 4 percent is used. Although affordability analyses often focus on median household incomes, this study stresses the use of incomes that more realistically represent the financial condition of low-income customers. Four types of monthly income (for families of different sizes) are considered: Aid to Families with

Table 4.4

Conservation and socioeconomic impacts of pricing strategies

Conservation pricing strategy	Conservation impact	Socioeconomic impact
Metering	Facilitates volume-based (variable) pricing for water services and enhances price signals; conservation may be limited if usage is not price-responsive.	Metering and submetering may raise affordability issues for some households.
Cost-based pricing	Sends an appropriate price signal about the value of water.	As costs and prices rise, affordability concerns also rise; price-responsive water uses may be curtailed.
Seasonal pricing	Can help lower usage during peak periods.	Allocates costs to peak users and more price-responsive usage.
Lifeline rates	Slightly weakens price signal for first block(s) of water usage; price of first block may be below marginal cost.	Improves affordability and retains conservation signal for higher blocks of water usage.
Monthly billing	Sends a more frequent price signal; provides water users with more information to adjust their usage.	Enhances water bill affordability; makes water billing cycle comparable to billing cycle for other utility bills and obligations

Dependent Children; Federal Supplemental Security Income; minimum wage; and federal poverty-level guidelines.

Income levels are compared to hypothetical base rates, which were derived by doubling the rates and services charges reported in a 1994 survey. Spreadsheet models were used to illustrate and evaluate the effects of different affordability rate models. The models allow for variations in: household size, monthly income, monthly water usage, monthly customer charge, water usage (low, average, or high), discount on usage, discount on total bill, and average usage for all households. The relative relationship of customer (fixed) and usage (variable) charges also was considered.

Five different income affordability models are considered (waiver of customer charge, discount usage rate, discount total bill, and two lifeline rates), as summarized in Table 4.5. Table 4.6 provides a summary of findings from the 17 spreadsheet illustrations generated for the report. Additional analyses of wastewater bill impacts also were presented separately.

Table 4.5

Five affordability rate models (AWWARF study)

Model	Description	Bill calculation
Model 1	A total waiver of the customer service charge offered only to low-income customers	Total bill = usage × usage rate
Model 2	A designated discount on the usage rate offered only to low-income customers	Total bill = customer charge + (65 percent usage rate × usage)
Model 3	A designated discount on the total bill offered only to low-income customers	Total bill = 0.8 [customer charge + (usage × usage rate)]
Model 4	A lifeline rate with three usage blocks, plus an inverted block rate structure made available to the entire residential class; the initial block is based on average usage for an average-sized household and priced at a discounted rate	Usage blocks 1 = 0 to 4.69 ccf 2 = 4.69 to 6.25 ccf 3 = > 6.25 ccf Total bill = Customer charge + [(75 percent usage rate × block 1 usage) + (usage rate × block 2 usage) + (125 percent usage rate × block 3 usage)]
Model 5	A lifeline rate with three usage blocks, plus an inverted block rate structure made available to the entire residential class; the initial block is based on average usage for households of a given size and priced at a discounted rate	Usage blocks 1 = 0 to 0.75 (household size × 2.5 ccf) ccf 2 = .75 (household size × 2.5 ccf) to (1.0 size × 2.5 ccf) 3 = > (household size × 2.5 ccf) Total bill = Customer charge + [(75 percent usage rate × block 1 usage) + (usage rate × block 2 usage) + (125 percent usage rate × block 3 usage)]

Source: Saunders et al. (1998).

Using these affordability models, managers can assess the extent to which socioeconomic characteristics of the service territory can present constraints on—or opportunities for—introducing a more progressive rate structure. For example, many smaller water systems serve only residential customers, which limits the ability of the utility to allocate costs to achieve efficiency and affordability goals. If the service population is poor and without income diversity, rate-design options that provide intraclass subsides will not be effective.

Table 4.6

Impact of water bills on low-income households: Summary of spreadsheet analyses in AWWARF study

	Household size	Income source	Income	Monthly usage (ccf)	Monthly customer charge	Usage charge	Baseline	Model 1	Model 2	Model 3	Model 4	Model 5
										Percentage of income		
1	1	Min. wage	$708	2.5	$8.58	$1.87	**1.9**	**0.7**	**1.6**	**1.5**	**1.7**	**1.7**
2	2			5.0			2.5	**1.3**	2.1	**2.0**	2.2	2.3
3	3			7.5			3.2	**2.0**	2.5	2.6	3.0	2.8
4	4			10.0			3.9	2.6	2.9	3.1	3.8	3.4
5	5			12.5			4.5	3.3	3.4	3.6	4.6	3.9
6	1	AFDC	$212	2.5			6.3	2.2	5.5	5.0	5.7	5.8
7	2		$294	5.0			6.1	3.2	5.0	4.9	5.4	5.5
8	3		$365	7.5			6.2	3.8	4.8	4.9	5.7	5.5
9	4		$435	10.0			6.3	4.3	4.8	5.0	6.2	5.5
10	5		$511	12.5			6.3	4.6	4.7	5.0	6.4	5.4
11	1	SSI	$446	2.5			3.0	**1.0**	2.6	2.4	2.7	2.8
12	2		$669	5.0			2.7	**1.4**	2.2	2.1	2.4	2.4
13	4	Min. wage	$708	15.0			5.2	4.0	3.8	4.1	5.4	5.0
14				5.0			2.5	**1.3**	2.1	**2.0**	2.2	2.2
15	2			7.5			3.2	**2.0**	2.5	2.6	3.0	3.1
16				2.5			**1.9**	**0.7**	**1.6**	**1.5**	**1.7**	**1.7**
17	3	AFDC	$366	7.5	$12.87	$0.94	5.4	**1.9**	4.8	4.4	5.2	5.1
18					$4.29	$2.81	6.9	5.8	4.9	5.5	6.3	5.9

Source: Adapted from Saunders et al. 1998, Appendix A.

Assumptions: Model 2 discount on usage rate = 35 percent.
Model 3 discount on total bill = 20 percent.
Model 4 first block's percentage of average usage = 75 percent.
Average usage for all households = 6.25 ccf (2.5 person household).
Bold indicates values falling at or below the 2 percent threshold.

SOCIOECONOMIC IMPACTS OF CONSERVATION PROGRAMS

As in the case of pricing, conservation programs also have distributional consequences. The costs and benefits of participation affect the income of the participant, although often less directly than prices. Programs that lower the cost of participation can improve participation rates and help spread the benefits of conservation throughout the service territory.

Different types of conservation measures that utilities might implement have potentially different socioeconomic consequences. Table 4.7 illustrates the range of possible socioeconomic impacts that might result from conservation programs. This list is not exhaustive; nor is it meant to suggest that impacts exist in each, or even most, cases. As a broad illustration, it shows that socioeconomic impacts might be positive or negative, large or small, and direct or indirect. A sizable direct and positive impact example is the impact of a direct install ultra-low-flush toilet (ULFT) in a low-income household. A sizable direct and negative impact is the introduction of submetering on low-income apartment dwellers who reside in older housing with leak-prone fixtures and no means of fixing them.

Many programs combine conservation measures. Rate changes, for example, often are used in conjunction with other programs to promote conservation. Multiple measures can have mixed socioeconomic effects. Thoughtful program design, however, can combine measures to maximize program effectiveness and mitigate undesirable outcomes.

Evaluating the socioeconomic impact of programmatic measures can be challenging. The analyst must take into account the influence of socioeconomic factors on the full range of factors that influence program costs and benefits. Important considerations for assessing program costs include

- *Participation rates.* For customer groups with low levels of language proficiency, literacy, education, and income, additional costs and program adaptations may be needed to achieve program participation. It may be beneficial to combine programs with social-service or other utility programs that already target certain customers.
- *Payback periods.* For customers strapped for cash, it may be important to ensure that customer payback periods are short enough to make economic incentives attractive. For utilities that are just gaining experience with conservation programs, programs with short payback periods may be easier to justify in the face of financial uncertainty.

Table 4.7

Water conservation measures and potential socioeconomic impacts

Category	Sample measure	Reduction in end use	Life span (years)	Potential socioeconomic impacts and issues
LEVEL 1 MEASURES				
Universal metering	Connection metering	20 percent	8 to 20	• Cost of metering paid by customers • Higher bills for customers with price-inelastic demand, with little reduction in usage • Can increase delinquency and disconnection • Can shift incentives for conservation (for example, from landlords to tenants)
	Submetering	20 to 40 percent	8 to 20	
Water accounting and loss control	System audits and leak detection	Based on system	na	• Reductions in total system costs can benefit all customers in the long term
Costing and pricing	10 percent increase in residential prices	2 to 4 percent	na	• Higher bills for customers with price-inelastic demand, with little reduction in usage • Tends to exacerbate regressiveness of utility bills.
	10 percent increase in nonresidential prices	5 to 8 percent	na	• Can have adverse impacts if large-volume customers leave the system
	Increasing-block rate	5 percent	na	• Higher bills for customers with price-inelastic demand, with little reduction in usage • Use of affordability criteria in designing first blocks can be beneficial to low-income customers
Information and education	Public education and behavior changes	2 to 5 percent	na	• Impacts can be positive or negative depending on program design (e.g, attention to socioeconomics)
LEVEL 2 MEASURES				
End-use audits	General industrial water conservation	10 to 20 percent	na	• Impacts can be positive or negative depending on program design (e.g, attention to socioeconomics) • Targeting to type of property is important
	Outdoor residential use	5 to 10 percent	na	
	Large landscape water audits	10 to 20 percent	na	

(continued)

Table 4.7 (continued)

Category	Sample measure	Reduction in end use	Life span (years)	Potential socioeconomic impacts and issues
LEVEL 2 MEASURES (continued)				
Retrofits	Toilet tank displacement devices (for toilets using > 3.5 gallons/flush)	2 to 3 gpcd	1.5	• Can be highly beneficial for low-income properties • Cost of participation can be a significant barrier (e.g., rebate program design) • Long-term effectiveness may vary with socioeconomic characteristics (e.g., removing fixtures)
	Toilet retrofit	8 to 14 gpcd	1.5	
	Showerhead retrofit (aerator)	4 gpcd	1 to 3	
	Faucet retrofit (aerator)	5 gpcd	1 to 3	
	Fixture leak repair	0.5 gpcd	1	
	Governmental buildings (indoors)	5 percent	na	
Pressure management	Pressure reduction, system	3 to 6 percent of total production	na	• Reductions in total system costs can benefit all customers in the long term
	Pressure-reducing valves, residential	5 to 30 percent	na	
Outdoor water-use efficiency	Low water-use plants	7.5 percent	10	• Impacts vary by property and ownership • Some risk of subsidy by low-income customers • Potential water savings may be greater in higher-income areas • Reductions in peak demand have systemwide benefits in the long term
	Lawn watering guides	15 to 20 percent	na	
	Large landscape management	10 to 25 percent	na	
	Irrigation timer	10 gpcd	4	
LEVEL 3 MEASURES				
Replacements and promotions	Toilet replacement, residential	16 to 20 gpcd	15 to 25	• Some programs may be very beneficial for low-income properties • Cost of participation can be a significant barrier (e.g., rebate program design) • Low-income properties have a lower saturation of water-using appliances and may not benefit
	Toilet replacement, commercial	16 to 20 gpcd	10 to 20	
	Showerhead replacement	8.1 gpcd	2 to 10	

(continued)

Table 4.7 (continued)

	Faucet replacement	6.4 gpcd	10 to 20	
Category	Sample measure	Reduction in end use	Life span (years)	Potential socioeconomic impacts and issues
LEVEL 3 MEASURES (continued)				
	Clothes washers, residential	4 to 12 gpcd	12	
	Dishwashers, residential	1 gpcd	12	
	Hot water demand units	10 gpcd	na	
Reuse and recycling	Cooling tower program	Up to 90 percent	na	• Reductions in total system costs can benefit all customers in the long term
Water-use regulation	Landscape requirements for new developments	10 to 20 percent in sector	na	• Benefits may be greater for higher income areas (new developments)
	Graywater reuse, residential	20 to 30 gpcd	na	
Integrated resource management	Planning and management	Energy, chemical, and wastewater treatment costs	na	• Reductions in total system costs can benefit all customers in the long term

Source: Authors' construct with measures and savings from U.S. Environmental Protection Agency, *Water Conservation Guidelines* (1998). Levels are used in the Guidelines to recognize the progressive and cumulative nature of conservation program activities for different types of water systems.

• *Benefits attribution.* Successful targeting can reduce the "free-rider" problem and allow for the proper attribution of water savings and financial benefits. Otherwise, a pitfall of conservation programs that try to mitigate socioeconomic impacts is the combined free-rider effect of both conservation and affordability program elements. In other words, targeting fails if well-off customers with efficient fixtures participate.

OBSERVATIONS

As the price of water rises to reflect true costs, utilities will have to be increasingly cognizant of the potential socioeconomic effects of changes in rates, rate structures, billing practices, and other factors. Underestimating how a change in policy or practice affects customers and particular customer groups can affect planned outcomes, as well as strain the relationship between the utility and the community it serves. Conservation has the goal of efficiency, but not the goal of curtailing usage that is necessary to sustain a safe, healthy, and comfortable lifestyle.

Like pricing, conservation programs can have meaningful socioeconomic consequences. Rebates and discounts for water-efficient fixtures, for example, have income or distributional effects similar to pricing. Costs to target or enhance participation effectively increase the cost of service, although these costs may be offset by program benefits (water savings) with reduced free-rider effects. Participation costs also affect participation rates by different customer groups and, therefore, the distribution of program benefits (including lower water bills that take a lower share of household income). As discussed in subsequent chapters, many utilities have incorporated socioeconomic considerations in their conservation programs, as well as their programs to address water affordability.

CHAPTER 5

SOCIOECONOMIC INFLUENCES ON PROGRAM EFFECTIVENESS

INTRODUCTION

This chapter focuses on the third of the three relationships defined by the conceptual model presented in chapter 2: How do socioeconomic characteristics of customers influence the effectiveness of utility programs in terms of achieving water conservation and other goals?

Socioeconomic variables intervene between utility programs and water use and conservation behavior on the part of customers. Understanding this linkage can help utilities design and implement more-effective programs. In important ways, this chapter builds on the analysis in the previous chapters and adds a more contextual dimension. Several case studies will illustrate utility programs that consider socioeconomic conditions, particularly income, in their conservation programs. The chapter also includes a discussion of the experiences of several utilities that have included conservation elements in programs to assist low-income and other customer groups. This framework is summarized in Table 5.1.

Utility conservation programs and utility affordability programs intersect in terms of socioeconomic impacts. Evidence suggests that conservation programs targeting the needs of the low-income population can both achieve water efficiency gains and enhance affordability. Likewise, affordability programs can, and often do, incorporate basic water conservation (or

Table 5.1

Types of utility programs

Program type	Targeting water usage	Targeting water price
Conservation	Audits, retrofits, information, and other forms of assistance to help reduce water usage (for example, toilet replacements)	
Affordability		Programs that provide a rate structure or rate discounts based on income or other needs criteria (for example, lifeline rates)
Hybrid	Programs that provide conservation assistance and/or require conservation activity as a condition of eligibility for a rate discount or other consideration	

"wise-use") principles. In practice, however, many utilities implement one program or the other—conservation or affordability—but not necessarily both. Even when utilities implement conservation programs and affordability programs, the extent of coordination varies.

As discussed previously, the water bill essentially is a product of water use and the rate charged for that water use. Conservation programs generally are aimed at the use component, and affordability programs generally are aimed at the rate component. Some programs have elements of both. In hybrid programs, conservation can be encouraged or required prior to eligibility for rate discounts.

CONSERVATION PROGRAMS ADDRESSING SOCIOECONOMIC ISSUES

This section provides an overview of several water utility conservation programs that incorporate socioeconomic considerations. In some cases, ongoing programs have been modified to target low-income customers so as to address special needs or to increase participation rates over rates occurring with existing efforts. These modifications reflect recognition on the part of utilities that the needs of low-income and other customer groups might require special attention when designing and implementing conservation programs.

Austin, Texas

In 1994, the City of Austin, Texas, implemented the Ultra Low-Flow Toilet Outreach Program to provide free toilets to residents in traditionally low-income zip code zones (Figure 5.1) who, because of the initial investment required, had not participated in the previous toilet rebate program (Poch 1995). Eligibility for the program takes into account family size and income, with different thresholds for residents under and over 60 years of age (see Table 5.2). The majority of program participants had incomes less than $25,000. Based on customer surveys, the vast majority of program participants (more than 90 percent) were pleased with city services, pleased with the store supplier, and satisfied with the low-flow toilet.

Analysts found that the program resulted in greater water savings than the rebate program (Figure 5.2). Taking into account toilets replaced, toilet leaks fixed, and showerheads replaced, the free toilet program achieved savings of 38.7 gallons per day—nearly 50 percent greater than

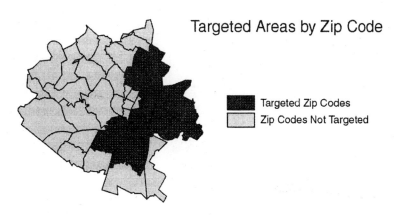

Targeted Areas by Zip Code

Targeted Zip Codes

Zip Codes Not Targeted

Source: Doxsey and McNabb 1998.

Figure 5.1   Targeted toilet-replacement program (Austin)

Table 5.2

Income eligibility criteria for Austin's ultra-low-flow outreach program

	Under age 60	Age 60 or older
1 person	$17,700	$25,150
2 persons	$17,950	$28,750
3 persons	$20,200	$32,350
4 persons	$22,400	$35,000
5 persons	$24,250	$38,800
6 persons	$26,050	$41,650
7 persons	$27,880	$44,440

Source: Doxsey and McNabb 1998.

savings achieved under the conventional program. Free ridership for the targeted program also was found to be much less than for the convention program (about 10 percent compared to 30 percent, respectively).

The city anticipated replacing a total of 15,000 toilets under the outreach program, which would achieve water savings (and reductions in wastewater flows) of 580,500 gallons per day at a total value of $41 million (based on a cost of $.005/gallon).

Denver, Colorado

In 1994, the Denver Water Department awarded a contract to the nonprofit Energy Conservation Association to conduct water audits and provide retrofits to low-income single-family

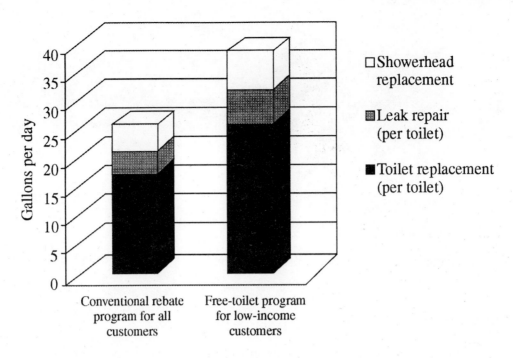

Source: Poch 1995.

Figure 5.2   Comparison of savings from conventional rebate and targeted free-toilet programs (Austin)

customers (Gallegos and Hernandez 1995). Funding is leveraged with other sources of support, and customers are provided a comprehensive set of services.

Three progressive water conservation steps were implemented: reduce, repair, and replace. The first stage (reduce) consisted of methods of detecting leaks, measuring flow and retrofit, and educating the customer. The second stage (repair) included replacements and adjustments to fixtures where waste was obvious. The third stage (replace) involved replacing faucets and toilet fixtures that were found to be beyond repair or functionally obsolete.

Analysts found the program to be highly cost-effective. Water saved at a cost of $1,400 to $2,400 per acre-foot was compared to a cost of $4,000 to $5,000 for conventional water supply options (Table 5.3).

Los Angeles, California

In a 1991 customer survey, the City of Los Angeles learned that poor customers are receptive to conservation programs but less likely to participate than wealthier customers (Pollyea

Table 5.3

Benefit-cost assessment of Denver's low-income conservation program

	1994–1995 program year	1995–1996 program year (estimates)
Cost per single-family home	$52	$140
Number of participating homes	326	900
Annual water savings	3.9 million gallons (12 acre-feet)	18.9 million gallons (58 acre-feet)
Cost per acre-foot	$1,400	$2,400
Conventional supply cost per acre-foot	$4,000 to $5,000	

Source: Gallegos and Hernandez 1995, 761–764.

1993). The Department of Water and Power designed a conservation program to target customers on the system's low-income water rate, as well as senior citizens and disabled customers who met income requirements. Total budget for the program was approximately $220,000, including the cost of a contractor hired for program management.

The program consisted of three mailings to 60,000 customers over a 10-week period: (1) a program announcement mailed first class, (2) a conservation kit mailed at bulk rates one week later, and (3) an assistance offer mailed first class two weeks later. Based on a follow-up survey,

- 87 percent of the targeted customers received the kits.
- 70 percent installed the shower head and left it in (36,540 showerheads).
- 33 percent installed two toilet displacement bags and 22 percent installed one toilet displacement bag (45,960 bags).

The contractor' office, which was open for 19 weeks during the program, was contacted by 2,900 participants for assistance in installing the conservation devices. This represents a response rate of 4.8 percent.

Philadelphia, Pennsylvania

The Philadelphia Water Department was among the first to initiate a targeted conservation program (Beecher 1994). A pilot program in 1986, which involved several hundred households,

71

was designed specifically to reduce the number of low-income households threatened with disconnection from water service because of nonpayment. The department has taken an active role in conservation, with a self-proclaimed "see a leak, fix a leak" posture. Modern plumbing efficiency and waste-reduction practices are emphasized, but the consumer orientation for the 1994-to-1997 program year is summarized in Figure 5.3 (Tollen, not dated).

A full-service, whole-house perspective is taken to jointly promote energy and water efficiency savings. Low-income properties are targeted because of the need to lower bills and the potential savings associated with replacing substandard fixtures. Success in Philadelphia is attributed to a community-based approach using the existing neighborhood energy centers (NECs) rather than creating a new service delivery infrastructure. Some program cost savings are realized by using skilled handymen instead of licensed plumbers.

The pilot program was evaluated in 1989 and was considered a success (see Table 5.4). Included in the findings are implications for customers' ability to pay. In general, customers whose bills remained steady or declined demonstrated significant improvements in paying bills. Another finding was that improvements in payment were better for customers with lower total bills. The majority of low-income customers were unable to pay their water bills in full when the

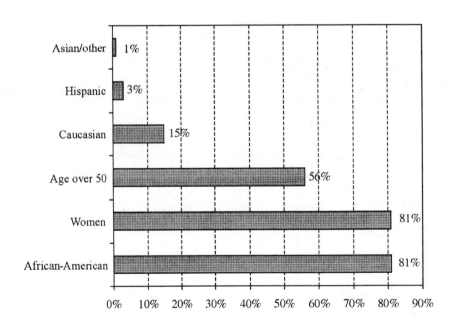

Source: Data provided by Philadelphia Water Department.

Figure 5.3   Profile of participating customers (Philadelphia)

72

Table 5.4

Philadelphia's targeted conservation program

Background	• The Philadelphia Water Department pilot is a program in which Water Department and NEC staff identified low-income clients who currently were payment-troubled or in danger of becoming so.
	• Participating customers could not have a household income exceeding 150 percent of the federal poverty level.
	• Participating customers could not have water-payment arrearages exceeding $2,000.
	• NEC crews inspected each house and listed needed repairs on an audit and intake form, which was used to define a preset cost limit for needed repairs.
	• NEC crews installed water-saving devices (including toilet dams, faucet aerators, and low-flow showerheads), repaired plumbing leaks, and educated homeowners about ways to reduce water use.
	• Households needing extensive plumbing repairs were referred to programs sponsored by other federal or local agencies.
Findings	• Approximately two-thirds (62 percent) of the 390 households evaluated realized significant reductions in daily water consumption.
	• Savings for the entire group (savers and losers together) averaged 9.1 cubic feet per day (68 gallons per day, or 3.7 thousand cubic feet per year).
	• Overall water consumption for the entire study group of 390 households was 25.8 percent lower in the post-treatment year. The median percentage savings was 19.7 percent of pretreatment consumption.
	• The resulting average reduction in annual billed costs is $50 per household.
	• Total contractor program costs averaged $90 per participant in this sample ($53 installation, $30 audit and intake, and $7 education materials), for a simple payback of 22 months ($90/$50).
	• Average water-heating energy savings were estimated at 4.3 million BTUs, yielding additional possible savings of $80 for gas or $150 for electricity.
	• The analysis probably significantly underestimated the total impact of the program measures of water consumption in many of the houses, because of limitations in the available data caused by meter-reading practices.
	• Although changes in payment behavior could not be fully analyzed, a clear improvement in average payment behavior was observed for customers whose bills actually reflected the effect of conservation improvements.
Conclusions	• The pilot program was considered a success in attaining significant usage reduction in a large number of participating households and was cost-effective.
	• Better results can be expected in other neighborhoods.
	• Lowered bills can lead to improved bill payment in most customers. A pilot program is recommended to incorporate counseling in budget and bill payment to maximize this improvement.
	• More frequent meter readings are necessary, both for more accurate evaluation and to enhance water conserving and bill paying by program participants.
	• Follow-up on the households that showed no change or an increase in water consumption after treatment should be done to provide information to further improve the program.

Source: Adapted from Lent (1989) and related summary materials.

total bill went beyond about $300 per year. Program administrators emphasized the goal of increasing customer understanding and satisfaction by various means, including more accessible and readable materials on water conservation.

Phoenix, Arizona

Phoenix considered implementing a targeted subsidy rate for low-income customers but has not adopted this option because it would be costly, would be inequitable, and would fail to encourage water-use efficiency (Babcock 1995). Instead, the City developed four programs to assist low-income residents in achieving a high degree of water efficiency:

1. Utilization of customer service field representatives and investigators as couriers of the conservation message.
2. Expansion of a program to assist seniors in energy conservation.
3. Funds to help pay summer utility bills for low-income residents.
4. A program offering audits, plumbing repair, and low-flow toilets to inner-city neighborhoods.

San Antonio, Texas

The "Plumbers to People" program is designed to address water conservation opportunities for low-income customers in the San Antonio Water System service area in San Antonio, Texas (Bohne 1995). The City estimated that fully a quarter of its population (225,000) live in poverty, often in housing more than 50 years old, and would benefit from an assistance program. Customer service personnel recognized rising water rates, the inability to pay for costly repairs, and an increasing threat of disconnection as growing concerns.

The company forged a partnership with the City of San Antonio Department of Community Initiatives, Community Action Division, to screen applicants eligible for assistance. Target groups, in order of priority, are

- Low-income elderly customers
- Low-income disabled customers

74

- Low-income families with young children
- Low-income families with unemployed heads of households
- Families demonstrating unavailability of resources in the 30 days prior to the application.

The goal of the program is to increase water conservation by eliminating leaks that otherwise would not be repaired because of the cost. Eligible customers can receive up to $400 in water leak repairs (up to $800 for senior citizens). The average cost per repair has been found to be $225, producing estimated water savings of about 27,000 gallons per household annually.

ASSISTANCE PROGRAMS ADDRESSING CONSERVATION

Water conservation can be, and often is, linked to other assistance programs offered to customers in need. As discussed earlier in this chapter, targeted conservation is one of the methods that water utilities can implement to assist customers who have difficulty paying their water bill. Conservation reduces the cost of water to customers and eliminates the need for subsidies from the utility.

Conservation can be a voluntary or a mandatory component of an assistance program. Voluntary programs provide customers with information and tools to reduce their water usage. Mandatory programs require customers to reduce usage in order to qualify for assistance.

The programs reviewed in this section have included conservation as part of their affordability programs. In addition, some of the utilities discussed have general or targeted conservation programs.

American Water Works Company

The operating companies of the American Water Works Company have implemented a number of programs to assist low- and fixed-income customers (Table 5.5). Customers are provided with conservation information along with other forms of assistance, including rate discounts and arrearage forgiveness for qualifying customers in some areas. The companies frequently form partnerships with local social assistance agencies to help administer assistance. In some cases, voluntary contributions from customers are used to help fund assistance efforts.

Table 5.5

American Water Works Company's customer assistance programs

Company	Program	Features
California: American Water Company	Program for Alternative Rates (PAR)	• Eliminates monthly meter charge for fixed low-income customers; customer pays only the variable portion of the bill. • Includes a water revenue adjustment mechanism to address increased revenue variability. • California law (section 739.8 (b)) provides for consideration by rate regulators of "programs to provide rate relief for low income rate payers."
Pennsylvania: American Water Company	Several programs, including tariff, arrearage-forgiveness, and conservation information	• Tariff discounts water bills for all qualifying customers. Service charge is discounted by 15 percent. • Voluntary funds from customers of $1, $3, or $5 are matched by shareholders, and are used for arrearage-forgiveness program. • Customers cannot miss more than one payment during any six-month enrollment. • Revenue losses are recovered from all customers, based on the system-wide benefit of reduced collection expenses.
Ohio: American Water Company	H$_2$O Help and Water Doctor	• Provides assistance to customers in jeopardy of disconnection. • Funded through voluntary customer contributions of $1 matched by shareholders up to $5,000. • Water Doctor assists senior citizens in leak detection and conservation.
West Virginia: American Water Company	Helping Hand	• Assists qualified customers with paying bills. • Eligibility based on State Department of Health and Human Services criteria. • Funded through voluntary customer contributions of $1 matched by shareholders up to $4,000.
Illinois: American Water Company	Project Help	• Assists customers in need with paying bills. • Funded through voluntary customer contributions of $1 to $99 matched by shareholders up to $25,000 without cost recovery. • Salvation Army administers the fund.
Tennessee: American Water Company	Project Water Help and billing cycle coordination	• Assists customers in need with paying bills. • Funded through voluntary customer contributions of $1. • United Way administers the fund. • Bill payment dates can be coordinated for fixed-income customers to coincide with social security or pension checks.

Source: Adapted from Pape 1998.

New York City

New York's ambitious toilet replacement program recognized the need to target low-income housing (including multifamily housing) because of the potential to save water and improve affordability. The City also provides a cap on metered charges based on customer participation in a conservation program that includes inspections, water-use audits, and the low-flow toilet retrofit program (Table 5.6).

Philadelphia Suburban Water Company

In early 1994, the Philadelphia Suburban Water Company proposed a Pilot Customer Assistance Program (PCAP) targeted to a county where uncollectible accounts were most problematic. A county assistance agency was used to run the program (including interviews, training, and oversight of repairs) while the company provided oversight, control, monitoring, and review functions. The company reports that the use of outside agencies for administration reduces the need for bureaucracy within the company and simplifies implementation.[*]

More than 400 households have benefited from the program, which has been expanded to all of the counties served by the utility. Participating customers are provided with (1) a water-use audit, (2) water conservation devices, (3) educational materials, (4) monthly billing and bill counseling, (5) payment agreements including arrearage-forgiveness opportunities, and (6) remote meters for consumption monitoring. To qualify for arrearage forgiveness, customers participating in the Helping Hand program must reduce water usage by 10 percent.

Of the program's many features, managers noted that monthly billing provides a significant source of relief. Initially, the company believed that monthly billing would be needed only temporarily, but many customers expressed a preference to continue paying monthly. In effect, the program evolved as a budget-billing plan. Monthly billing makes the size of the water bill more manageable and also places it in a payment cycle comparable to other bills in households (Table 5.7).

---

[*] Interview with Rob Roberson, Philadelphia Suburban Water Company, December 1998.

Table 5.6

New York City's cap on metered charges and conservation provisions

1. A residential premise receiving metered water and/or sewer service shall be eligible to have its metered water and/or sewer charges limited to a maximum amount, as set forth herein. The maximum metered charge shall apply to all routine domestic use of water and/or sewer service and shall not apply to excessive use of irrigation, commercial processes, or recreational activities, which shall be billed in accordance with the metered rate set forth in Part II, Section 1 hereof. A metered residential premise shall be eligible to have a maximum-metered charge imposed, if it meets the following conditions:

   a. a request is made in writing to BWEC [Bureau of Water and Energy Conservation] within one year of the date of entry on the meter bill;

   b. the property owner agrees to have DEP [Department of Environmental Protection] perform a water survey within six months of application, and if such a survey indicates that a leak or waste condition exists, then the property owner agrees to take all reasonable measures to eliminate such conditions within thirty (30 days);

   c. the property owner permits access to the property for the installation, repair, replacement, or inspection of a meter or a remote reading device;

   d. the property owner agrees to participate in the DEP Low-Flow Toilet Retrofit Rebate Program, or at least seventy percent (70 percent) of the toilets in the premise are low-flow toilets that meet the standards of Local Law 29 (1989) and at least seventy percent (70 percent) of the showerheads are low-flow devices, and substantially all of the faucets are equipped with faucet aerators and such installations or replacements have been approved by the Commissioner; and

   e. if the premise is a multiple family building, then the building manager or owner agrees to participate in the Water Conservation Seminar sponsored by DEP and the NYC Department of Housing Preservation and Development within six months of application.

2. The maximum metered charge for any residential premise in any billing period shall be equal to the charges imposed for metered consumption of 78.43 cubic feet (CF) per day for the first dwelling unit in the premise and 52.28 CF per day for each additional dwelling unit, multiplied by the number of days covered by the metered bill and the water and/or sewer rates in effect during such period.

   Maximum Meter Charge Illustration

   For first residential unit (equal to annual water and sewer charge of $750):

   Maximum annual charge = maximum annual CF * rate per CF

   Maximum annual CF = maximum annual charge/rate per CF

   Maximum annual CF = $750/$0.0262 = 28,626 CF

   Maximum CF per day = 28,626/365 days = 78.43 CF per day

   For each additional residential unit (equal to annual water and sewer charge of $500):

   Maximum annual CF = $500/$0.0262 = 19,084

   Maximum CF per day = 19,084/365 days = 52.28 CF per day

3. Notwithstanding the provisions of this Part, section 3, paragraph 1a, that requires an application for a maximum metered charge be made within one year of the date of entry of the metered bill, in the case of residential premises having service lines of less than one-and-one half (1.5") in diameter, the maximum metered charge as set forth herein shall apply to all service provided after July 1, 1988.

Source: New York City Water Board Water and Sewer Rate Schedule, Effective July 1, 1993, 27–9.

Table 5.7

Philadelphia Suburban Water Company's Helping Hand Program

Introduction

A Helping Hand (AHH) is a low-income assistance program developed by the Philadelphia Suburban Water Company (PSW) that was launched as a pilot last year. It is the first low-income assistance offered by any investor-owned water utility in the Commonwealth. A consultant's evaluation of this pilot was recently completed and submitted to the Public Utility Commission (PUC) (complete copies of the report are available upon request).

AHH, which was administered by the Company with the assistance of the Community Action Agency of Delaware County (CAADC), was designed to reduce the water usage and customer arrearages of low-income, payment-troubled customers. Three hundred and thirty-five (335) customers were entered into the pilot program.

AHH was found to:

- help make water service more affordable to low-income customers;
- provide a more cost-effective means of collections than traditional approaches;
- conserve water.

The pilot was very successful, and AHH has now become part of PSW's overall commitment to quality customer service.

Program Description

The key components of AHH are that:

- it is targeted to low-income (150 percent of poverty), payment-troubled customers;
- water usage reduction is encouraged through a water conservation program including education, the installation of water conservation devices, and plumbing repairs;
- regular payments are encouraged through monthly billing (rather than quarterly); monthly payments of $5, $10, or $15 are required to reduce arrearages; forgiveness can be earned by meeting the payment obligations (up to $50 in forgiveness is earned after meeting this obligation for six months) and by reducing water consumption by 10 percent over the first six months (an additional arrearage forgiveness of up to $25 is earned if this target is also met); and
- charitable contributions from our customer base is encouraged through donations to a low-income assistance fund, and solicited through bill inserts.

AHH was offered to eligible customers in a pilot area of PSW's service territory in the southern end of Delaware County. This region contains about 39 percent of PSW's customers and about 54 percent of its arrearages older than 60 days.

AHH was administered with the assistance of the CAADC, which was responsible for contacting payment-troubled customers identified by PSW, screening applicants, and performing a home visit, which included a water-usage audit, water conservation education, and the installation of water conservation devices. PSW did not build an internal bureaucracy, as the CAADC proved to be very effective.

The conservation measures included: education; installing aerators, low-flow showerheads, toilet tank restrictors, and fluid masters; replacing washers, flapper valves, toilet floats, and toilet guide rods; and other miscellaneous plumbing repairs.

(continued)

Table 5.7 (continued)

Pilot Results

The pilot program was evaluated to provide an understanding of the ongoing costs and benefits of the program. The major findings of the pilot's evaluation are listed below.

1. PSW was firmly committed to make this program work, and went the extra mile to assist customers with the program to assure success. PSW made many modifications during the pilot period to improve the process.

2. Teaming with a capable community-based organization, rather than building an internal bureaucracy, was an extremely valuable component to the success of the program.

3. AHH met all of the cost-effectiveness tests to which it was subjected.

4. Water usage was reduced by low-income customers by about 20 percent.

5. The conservation services were cost-effective, with a 1 to 4.5 year payback.

6. AHH increased affordability of water bills as measured by an increase in percentage of bills paid from 76 percent to 86 percent.

7. Arrearages of the average pilot participant decreased by $82.

8. For a one-time investment of $85 per participant, PSW received an increase in revenues paid by the customer of $39 to $51 annually.

9. Program administration costs can be further streamlined, making the program even more attractive.

PSW's belief that it makes more sense to spend about $100 for conservation than to write off thousands of dollars incurred through waste has been supported by the results of this pilot.

Next Steps

The program was a success but still has room for improvement. It is, therefore, recommended that AHH be continued, subject to the following guidelines:

1. AHH should be expanded system wide, but only where strategic partners such as CAADC or other similar community-based organizations can be identified.

2. The roles of community-based organizations should be expanded to include program compliance monitoring, follow-up, and budget counseling.

3. Customer solicitation/enrollment for AHH should be included as a standard part of the collections process.

4. The requirement that customers call in monthly meter readings to remain in the program should be dropped. Monthly bills should be issued based on estimates between quarterly read cycles.

5. A waiver should be sought from any PUC regulation that may prohibit the issuance of monthly bills based upon estimated data as part of this program.

6. More flexible eligibility standards will be considered, with priority given to PSW customers who are in arrears.

7. To reduce cost of delivering conservation services, an effort should be undertaken to try to coordinate AHH with PECO Energy and its Low-Income Usage Reduction Program (LIURP).

Source: Philadelphia Suburban Water Company, "A Helping Hand: A Low-income Assistance Program, Pilot Program Evaluation Executive Summary" (not dated).

Portland, Oregon

The City of Portland implements a number of water conservation programs (Lifeline Rate Committee 1997). A pilot study in Portland found that between 5 and 6 percent (6,000 to 7,000) of total residential customer accounts were estimated to meet primary screening criteria (1) within a $27,000 income threshold; (2) high use (150 percent of winter average); and (3) occupying a single-family residence.

Although participants were selected because of their high water use, only 18 percent of the respondents viewed their use as "high." The majority thought their use was "average," and about 25 percent of the respondents thought their usage was at a "low" level.

Initial speculation was that the high water use was caused by (1) property-side leaks; (2) leaking plumbing fixtures in the house; and (3) lifestyle habits and conditions. The pilot study, however, indicated that lifestyle choice (primarily family size) was the most influential factor. Leaking fixtures were also an influence; property-side leaks were not.

The City's program combines bill relief and demand reduction. The bill-relief elements include crisis assistance, a low-income discount, and budget billing. The demand-reduction elements include self-help workshops to teach water use efficiency and simple plumbing-fixture repairs, conservation-kit distribution, information dissemination that networks with low-income assistance agencies, and a fixture-repair program that funds materials and/or labor costs for minor fixture repairs (repairs costing less than $500) (Dietz and Ranton 1995).

NON-INCOME CONSIDERATIONS

Language

In many communities, language presents a barrier to participating in water conservation and other programs. Depending on the demographic makeup of the community, utilities should consider providing conservation materials in Spanish or other languages as appropriate.

Bilingual water auditors and customer service personnel can improve participation rates and program effectiveness. "Protector Del Agua," for example, is a successful bilingual water conservation program in the Water Conservation Office of the California Department of Water Resources, designed to involve the Spanish-speaking population in water conservation (Caravajal 1993).

The low-income conservation programs in Los Angeles and Phoenix provide materials in English and Spanish. Water utilities also should be sensitive to cultural and ethnic diversities in their service population. Although systematic empirical evidence showing the effect of culture and ethnicity on water use and conservation is not readily available, these traits—along with language—may affect customer participation in utility programs. Water utilities can work with community leaders and organizations to address special needs within their service territories.

Multifamily Housing

Some water conservation programs include provisions to target activities toward multi-family structures. The rationale for targeting multifamily dwellings in older communities is that leakage rates can be high and fixtures often are older and less efficient than replacement models. Programs targeted toward multifamily dwellings also can help lower costs and rents to households, including in particular low-income households. New York's highly successful toilet rebate program included targets for multifamily housing.

Programs for multifamily dwellings tend to target some materials to residents and some to landlords or maintenance personnel. Phoenix provides a brochure, "The Renter's Guide to Saving Water and Money," both in English and Spanish (Table 5.8), which targets indoor water usage. Programs in Tucson provide property owners and maintenance staff with indoor and outdoor audits and suggestions for applying Xeriscape (low water use for landscaping) principles (Little and Waterfall 1990).

Public housing facilities may present unique opportunities, as well as unique challenges, for water savings. A 1989 demonstration program by the Lower Colorado River Authority experienced few implementation problems (even in older housing stock) and a high degree of customer acceptance (Mullarkey 1991). Multifamily housing developers may face strong market-based incentives to conserve water in new projects (Iadarola et al. 1995). In some service areas, higher tap fees associated with higher expected water use make it in the best interest of the developer to be as efficient as possible.

Table 5.8

Indicios de carencia o exceso de agua

Exceso
- La tierra está constantemente humeda
- Las hojas se vuelven menos verdosoas o amarillentas
- Los retoños están marchitos
- Las hojas están verdes pero quebradizas
- Cuando hay hongos o algas

Carencia
- La tierra está seca
- Las hojas viejas se tornan amarillas, cafes y se caen
- Las hojas están marchitas
- Las hojas están torcidas

Sugerencias para regar eficientemente
- Aplique de 3 a 4 pulgadas de pajote debajo del toldo de la planta. El pajote retiene la humedad e impide el crecimeinto de hierbas.
- No cubra la tierra con plástico.
- Evite rociar los árboles o plantas con agua. El agua contiene sales que pueden ser dañinas al follaje.
- Controle las yerbas, inclusive en áreas de césped, ya que estas compiten por el agua que les da a sus plantas.
- Si riega a mano, instale un medidor de tiempo en la llave del agua y use una manguera perforada de empapamineto.
- Una o dos veces al año, riegue dos veces más largo que lo normal para asistir en extraer las sales del sistema de raices.
- Riegue más espacio en cuanto más crece su planta.
- Prevenga desperdicio de agua! Retenga el agua en una depresión alrededor de su planta o riegue más despacio.

Para más informacion:
Cominiquese con el Departamento de Servicios de Agua del la Ciudad de Phoenix para otras ideas de como conservar agua en su hogar. 212-6251

Source: Phoenix Water Department, "Indicios de Carencia o Exceso de Agua," El Riego de los Arboles y Arbustos (undated brochure).

A study of an apartment building retrofit in Tampa, Florida, summarized in Figure 5.4, found significant reductions in average and especially maximum water use (Nero, Mulville-Fiel, and Anderson 1993):

- The apartment units retrofitted with low water consumption fixtures realized a 15.6-gallons/day/apartment, or 17 percent, reduction in water use, which translated into an 11-gallons per-person per-day reduction.

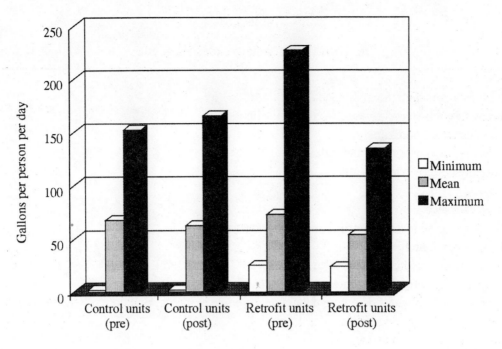

Source: Nero, Mulville-Fiel, and Anderson 1993.

Figure 5.4 Apartment retrofit results (Tampa)

- User acceptance of the low water consumption fixtures at the apartments was generally positive. The variation between the retrofit group and the control group in terms of tenant opinions about the adequacy of toilets and fixtures was not considered significant (less than 7 percent).

- Retrofit-group respondents using new fixtures reported less multiple flushing and less frequent toilet clogging than control-group respondents using conventional fixtures.

- A few tenants complained about the adequacy and hygiene of the retrofit toilets. A few tenants also complained about the retrofit showerheads and planned to remove them.

- Apartment complex maintenance personnel reported no unusual maintenance requirements or problems with the retrofit fixtures.

Family Size

When crafting policies and programs, a few utility programs consider family size. As noted earlier, analysts in Portland have found that family size is a lifestyle variable that significantly influences water use.

Conservation-oriented water rates can have adverse effects on large families with high levels of indoor water use for basic consumption and sanitation needs. The City of Los Angeles is among the few water utilities taking into account family size—along with lot size and temperature zone—in its rate structure. The two-tiered, increasing-block rate applies the first-tier rate to an allowed usage amount. Figure 5.5 illustrates how the amount of usage varies according to household size. While the price signals embedded in the rate are maintained, the threshold at which second-tier rates apply increases with family size.

Customer's Age

Many water conservationists believe that youths hold the key to a long-term commitment to water conservation. Youth education reflects the perception that shaping the perspective and water-use habits of young people might be easier than changing the perspectives and habits of adults, as well as have more-lasting effects. Many utility conservation programs include a youth-education

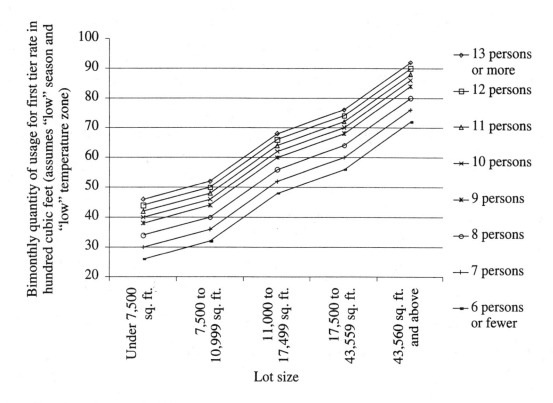

Source: Los Angeles rate tariff.

Figure 5.5   Consideration of family size in Los Angeles water rates

85

component that helps take the conservation message home and encourages wise water use on the part of future water consumers.

An example of a comprehensive youth-education program is "Learning to be Water Wise and Energy-Efficient," which is offered to more than 55,000 fifth-grade students in the Texas upper gulf coast areas including Harris, Galveston, and Fort Bend Counties, Texas (Baker 1995). The program combines an education curriculum that teaches how to consume less water and energy by combining high-efficiency plumbing equipment and new water-smart habits.

Each participating student and teacher receives a water conservation instructional materials package that teaches a number of behaviors to alter wasteful habits, as well as a kit that includes a low-flow showerhead, low-flow kitchen and bathroom aerators, water/rain gauge, water heater temperature check device, and leak-detection tablets. Each unit is designed specifically to give teachers, parents, and students the "hands-on" experience of installing and monitoring water and energy conservation equipment. With parents' help, the students install the devices and complete home energy checkups. The program is grounded in the belief that school children can influence their parents' water and energy use patterns quickly and effectively.

A few water utilities provide discounts and other programs for senior citizens, based primarily on the rationale that seniors are on fixed incomes. The Ohio-American Water Company implements a program known as "Water Doctor," which provides leak-detection and conservation assistance to senior citizens (Pape 1998). Many utility education programs involve senior citizens as well. Utilities often provide educational materials and presentations to community organizations representing seniors. Senior groups also sometimes participate in distributing conservation kits.

Forced Conservation? The Use of Flow Restriction

An unconventional and somewhat controversial alternative to disconnection involves installing a device that restricts the flow of water at a customer's residence. Water flow can be restricted to a fraction of the normal rate, depending on system pressure, as well as pipe and meter sizes. Water pressure to the premises is unaltered and unaffected.

Flow restriction is different from flow regulation. Flow-restricting devices allow delivery of enough water for basic drinking and sanitation needs. The water flow allowed through a restrictive device can be too limited for operating many appliances, watering lawns, taking normal showers, or using second-story fixtures. Even for sanitary purposes (bathing and toilet flushing), the low rate of water flow can be time-consuming. The use of more than one water fixture at a time is virtually precluded. In theory, although considerably inconvenient to customers, flow restriction is a humane alternative to complete disconnection. In effect, flow restriction constitutes a sanctioned degradation of water service quality comparable to an electricity service limiter.[*]

A related approach is prepaid metered usage where after an allowed amount, service is discontinued until another prepayment is made. Prepaid service is used in the telecommunications (especially wireless service) and energy sectors. Prepaid service could be used by water utilities, depending on metering, monitoring, and shut-off capability.

A utility in the Pacific Northwest serving 2,200 customers through 36 separate water systems has used a flow-restriction device for chronic nonpaying customers with a long history of both bad debt and refusal to cooperate with the utility (Beecher 1994). The company will work with hardship cases to maintain full water service; flow restriction is reserved for customers considered irresponsible and uncooperative. The device displaces the meter, costs about $25 to $30, and has an adjustable range of flow levels. A 1-gallon per minute flow rate is used. This compares to an unrestricted flow rate ranging between 15 and 30 gallons per minute.[†] For the typical household, the device motivates customers to pay and is not in place for long. Detailed statistics on the use of the device and its effectiveness in prompting bill payment have not been compiled.

Utility regulators have expressed concern about using flow restriction, but the company specifically suggested use of this measure as an alternative to disconnection for customers with chronic payment problems. Use of flow restriction was conditionally approved with the provision that utilities present to customers as an option. Flow restriction as a matter of policy raises a variety of issues, particularly with respect to the limited conditions under which its use may be appropriate (Miller et al. 1992). Use of the device may appear to be a rather Orwellian solution: a government-sanctioned and unwelcome intrusion on the common person's well-being. The choice

---

[*] Baltimore Gas and Electric Company uses a kilowatt restriction device that triggers a circuit breaker when electricity customers exceed allowed use. Flow restriction is not used in the natural gas sector because of public safety considerations.

[†] A restricted rate of .5 gallons per minute had been tried, but clogging stopped the flow altogether and resulted in additional service calls. A somewhat unanticipated consequence of the .5 rate, however, was that it facilitated leak detection on the premises. At a severely restricted flow rate, a leak will divert much of the water from its intended use.

of disconnection versus flow restriction also has the appearance of a "devil's choice" for customers.

Flow restriction may be viewed as more humane in relative terms (relative to disconnection) but not necessarily a humane option in absolute terms. Utilities must recover the cost of installing and removing the device either from the restricted customer or from other utility customers. Another controversial policy issue raised by flow restriction is the potential application to perceived water wasters for forced conservation, particularly during periods of shortage.

In California, for example, rules regarding the use of flow-restriction devices are part of the mandatory rationing plan specified in the Public Utilities Commission's tariff schedule regarding water emergencies. During recent drought experience in the state, the threat of installing the device may have served as a deterrent to some customers who otherwise might have violated rationing provisions (Beecher 1994). No devices actually were installed, however, in part because of resistance to their use by California water utilities. Generally, existing utility tariffs do not provide for installing flow-restrictive devices or for device removal and restoration of full service.

LESSONS LEARNED

The available evaluation studies of select utility experiences with targeted water conservation programs generally report positive utility experiences and results (Table 5.9). With few exceptions, water savings and cost savings are achieved that directly benefit the targeted population. Assistance programs including a conservation component also report positive results.

Utility programs can consider a growing number of socioeconomic variables. Although income will continue to be the focus of programs aimed at alleviating cost pressures, additional dimensions that might be considered in designing conservation and assistance efforts include language, housing, and age.

A need may exist for further coordination of programs designed for conservation purposes and programs designed for assistance purposes. In doing so, utilities can further both sets of goals.

Table 5.9

Overview of selected utility programs

	Program	Benefit(s)	Comments
Austin Water Department	Ultra Low Flush Toilet Program	Free toilets for eligible customers	More cost-effective than conventional rebate program
Denver Water	Low-income conservation program	Three stages: reduce, repair, replace	Services provided by the Energy Conservation Association
Los Angeles Water and Power	Targeted conservation	Customers on low-income rate received kits, follow-up contacts	Rate structure also considers family size
Philadelphia Water Department	Targeted conservation	Leak repair	Based on a 1986 pilot program
Phoenix Water Department	Targeted conservation	Audits, plumbing repair, and low-flow toilets to inner-city neighborhoods	Adopted in lieu of a rate subsidy
San Antonio	Plumbers to People	Low-cost plumbing repairs	Partner agency, Department of Community Initiatives, provides screening
American Water Works Company	Various assistance programs	Targeted discounts with conservation information	Some programs use voluntary contributions
New York City Water Department	Cap on metered charges	Requires participation in conservation programs	Toilet replacement program includes low-income and multifamily targets
Philadelphia Suburban Water Company	A Helping Hand	Provides conservation audits and training and monthly billing; customers must reduce usage by 10 percent; arrearage forgiveness up to $75	Began as a pilot program, now being extended; relies on social service agencies for implementation
Portland Water Department	Low-income program	Combines bill relief and demand reduction	Began with pilot study

CHAPTER 6
PLANNING AND EVALUATION METHODS

INTRODUCTION

As discussed throughout this report, the goal of water conservation can produce unintended impacts on customers at times. Conservation programs designed to be most "cost-effective" to meet economic objectives may be at odds with social equity goals. A focus on only "socio" or only "economic" indeed might allow optimization of a single objective, but it does not provide guidance on making decisions with different criteria. This chapter introduces a decision framework that planners and policy makers can use to jointly consider economic, equity, and other criteria in fulfilling their goals. The chapter then addresses how to adapt existing analytic methods to better understand the socioeconomic impacts of conservation programs and how knowledge of socioeconomic characteristics can improve planning.

PLANNING AND EVALUATION

Planning methods—the main emphasis of this chapter—are designed to provide forward-looking prospective information to decision makers who are considering strategy and investments. Evaluation methods are designed to look at the historical record of programs to provide retrospective information for administrators seeking to improve existing programs as well as decision makers considering future strategy and investments. The distinction between planning and evaluation becomes slim when the results of retrospective evaluation methods can be used for prospective planning purposes. In this chapter we focus attention on a framework and methods to improve planning strategy and investments based on the best possible information from all sources.

Decision Framework

A classic approach to analyzing public policy programs is to follow the basic steps of policy analysis:

1. Define the problem.
2. Select program goals.
3. Determine criteria to measure progress toward goals (such as net benefits, stakeholder equity, administrative efficiency, and political feasibility).
4. Compare alternatives.
5. Make recommendations.

Note that a focus only on the economic criteria will limit the analysis and narrow the methodology to quantified costs and benefits—to the neglect or exclusion of other potentially important criteria. A broader policy analytic approach can be designed to organize multiple criteria assessments even when the criteria are different in nature.

Defining the Problem

What is the problem we are trying to solve? This fundamental question may have different answers when we consider conservation in a larger context, to include socioeconomic impacts. Historically, the problem that conservation programs are trying to "fix" is that of fixed water resources in the face of growing demand driven by population and the economy. In recent years, this "supply-demand" problem has been exacerbated by environmental threats to water quality and, thus, to supply sources.

Consideration of the socioeconomic impacts of conservation programs has been stimulated by concerns that these programs may be exacerbating, or at least not improving, poverty conditions. Another "problem" that conservation might address is the economic cost to utilities of late payments and arrearages. Yet a third problem, or class of problems, has to do with the effectiveness and cost-effectiveness of conservation programs: Are conservation programs performing poorly because we do not have adequate knowledge of socioeconomic characteristics in our communities? Does this make it difficult or impossible to effectively target and design our programs? If we are setting out to solve a problem, the first step is to define the problem.

Evaluation Goals and Criteria

Only after defining the problem can program goals be selected to address that problem. In a practical policy-making context, goals should be achievable and provide broad guidance based on basic principles. Evaluation criteria provide measurable indicators of our progress—or lack thereof—toward goals.

These distinctions become concrete when we recall the conceptual framework in chapter 2, which identifies three relationships between conservation programs and socioeconomic characteristics and outcomes. In the first relationship, socioeconomic characteristics are understood as an input. That is, the socioeconomic characteristics of customers act as explanatory (independent) variables when modeling water use and conservation. In the second and third relationships, socioeconomic conditions are understood as outcomes.

The asymmetry of the terms input and outcome is purposive. In the framework for policy analysis, a distinction is made between outputs and outcomes. An output is what the policy system produces. An example is a water conservation rate. The output itself ensures no progress toward a goal or end result. The outcome is the end result, such as progress toward a program goal. In the case of the conservation rate (an output), one outcome might be a reduction in water use. But other outcomes might occur as well. For example, the customer's disposable income might be reduced by the amount that water bills increase. A more severe outcome might be an inability to pay the bill and disconnection. Have we then made progress toward our goals?

Understanding the actual outcomes of policy choices and seeing both their progress toward the selected goals and unintended consequences are important. Measurable indicators of progress toward goals (or unintended consequences) might include program outputs that serve as decision criteria.

Alternatives, Recommendations, and Tradeoffs

Often, program design and implementation can take several approaches. When crafting conservation policies, comparison of alternatives allows us to better understand the best course of action. Even if there is only one policy choice, at times the "no project" alternative serves as a base of comparison.

Decision criteria used to weigh the alternatives can be of diverse types—both qualitative and quantitative measures. How does one make tradeoffs when different criteria are assessed and lead to different conclusions? What happens when a low-income conservation program that advances equity goals does not look cost-effective in a standard economic analysis?

One first step might be to look harder to see more clearly the limits of the quantitative analysis. Are there benefits that simply have not been identified or quantified? For example, if the program reduces the need for welfare agency caseworkers, is this benefit identified? Only after a comprehensive identification of the important costs and benefits can we compare alternatives.

Second, one has to weigh the different conclusions drawn from different criteria. Then the necessary judgments must be made explicit, explaining their rationale, and this comparison presented to the decision makers for approval or rejection.

ANALYTIC METHODS

Given the diverse circumstances in which the socioeconomic impacts of conservation programs are assessed and planned, the "toolbox" of analytic methods has to contain more than just a hammer. As the adage goes, "If you have only a hammer, every problem looks like a nail." Table 6.1 summarizes a range of analytic tools that can be applied to a wide variety of questions and circumstances.

Descriptive Impact Assessment

Identify and describe how the alternatives rate with the selected criteria in terms of the alternatives' ability to fulfill goals and objectives. This method is often used when constraints on

94

Table 6.1

Summary of evaluation approaches

Approach	Description
Descriptive impact assessment	• Is used as a low-cost assessment tool • Can be used as a preliminary analysis or screening tool • Recognizes potential socioeconomic impacts in a given community • Does not attempt to formally quantify benefits or impacts • Requires little resources or data and not highly analytical or complex • May be useful for smaller communities • May produce too little information for systematic decision making
Impact ordering	• Is used to rank-order options according to generalized impacts • Is more systematic than simple descriptive analysis • Requires development of assessment criteria • Is not highly analytical or complex • May be useful for smaller or middle-sized communities • Can inform decision making to a degree
Cost-effectiveness analysis: socioeconomic impact as a constraint	• Is used to choose most cost-effective conservation option among those meeting socioeconomic impact criteria • Focuses on avoiding or minimizing adverse impacts • Socioeconomic considerations are used to narrow the range of options • Requires some data and analysis • May be useful for larger communities and those with significant socioeconomic issues • Does not require the dollar valuation of benefits
Cost-effectiveness analysis: efficiency as a constraint	• Is used to choose the most equitable conservation option among those meeting efficiency criteria • Focuses on achieving water savings through conservation • Efficiency considerations are used to narrow the range of options • Requires some data and analysis • May be useful for larger communities and those with significant water conservation needs • Does not require the dollar valuation of benefits
Formal benefit-cost analysis	• Is used to perform a quantitative assessment of socioeconomic impacts • Integrates consideration of efficiency and socioeconomic impacts • Incorporates socioeconomic considerations in a benefit-cost analysis • Does not preclude any options from consideration • Requires significant resources, data, and analysis • Requires the dollar valuation of all costs and benefits • May be useful for larger and diverse communities in the context of long-term resource planning • Many impacts are not readily quantifiable or valued in dollar terms

time, resources, or methods make it difficult to reliably quantify or analyze the issues, or as a first step in a more extensive analysis.

Impact Ordering

Apply judgments or order the degree to which alternatives fulfill the goals and objectives, as assessed by the criteria. Place ordinal judgments on their relative impact (for example, 1 to 10, high to low). As in descriptive impact assessment, this method is useful under constrained conditions.

Cost-Effectiveness Analysis: Socioeconomic Impacts as a Constraint

Cost-effectiveness analysis involves calculating the dollars per unit of an effectiveness measure, such as dollars per acre-foot of water conserved ($/acre-foot). By calculating the cost per acre-foot of various conservation measures, we can decide how to invest scarce conservation dollars to get the most bang for the buck.

When we are analyzing the socioeconomic impacts, we can use cost-effectiveness analysis in several says. One way is to place a "socioeconomic impacts constraint" on the selection of investments. This involves using cost-effectiveness analysis to identify cost-effective solutions for programs that are confined in terms of particular components or types of impacts. For example, we could ask the question, "What is the most conservation water savings we can get from an investment in an ULFT program, given that the program will not require low-income households to incur additional costs?" This framing points us in the direction of selecting, for example, among direct install options for low-income households, perhaps in combination with other program designs for all other households—such as a co-payment.

Cost-Effectiveness Analysis: Cost as a Constraint

Yet another way to frame the use of investment decisions that can be analyzed with cost-effectiveness analysis is to ask the question, "How much equity can we buy with a given budget?" In this case, the effectiveness measure (the "bang") is an output related to equity outcome. For example, we may call a process output the number of low-income households that get direct-install ULFT installations. What is the maximum number of installations that can be achieved with a constrained conservation budget? Alternatively, how can water savings be maximized with a fixed budget? Maximizing installations focuses attention on conservation program marketing (attaining cost-effective program scale, low-cost publicity); maximizing water savings focuses attention on where toilet replacements save the most water (customers with older toilets, customers with more residents using each toilet). These two objectives, of course, are interrelated.

Net-Benefit Analysis

In contrast to cost-effectiveness analysis, net-benefit analysis, or the analysis of net present value (NPV), puts both costs and benefits in quantitative monetary terms. This method has the advantage that, unlike costs and benefits, it can make comparisons in commensurate units. For example, one can compare whether the benefits of conservation (for example, avoided water supply costs) outweigh the costs of program design and implementation.

One also can sum unlike benefit categories to get a more comprehensive view of the benefits that we are comparing to costs. For example, we might add both the benefits of avoided water supply and the benefits of avoided social services costs that might accrue if the conservation program helps mitigate financial pressure for some low-income households. This is not to say that water conservation programs will eliminate social services costs, but that some share of social services costs may be reduced if financial pressure is reduced at the margin.

A final plus of a net-benefit analysis is that its primary result—"net benefits"—is a consistent economic measure upon which to base decisions. By NPV, we mean specifically the present value benefits minus the present value costs: PV Net Benefits = PV Benefits – PV Costs. Discounting the "streams" of costs and benefits into their equivalent present-day value over time arrives at present value into their equivalent present-day value.[*]

Although cost-effectiveness analysis also measures costs in present value terms, net benefits show us the magnitude of net benefits, not just the ratio of benefits to costs. Perhaps an alternative with large net benefits will be attractive compared to a smaller net benefits program that has a more

---

[*] The formula for discounting can be found in standard finance, engineering-economics, and cost-benefit textbooks.

favorable ratio of benefits to costs. Cost-benefit ratios also have the disadvantage that distinctions between costs and benefits are sometimes accounting conventions. Recategorizing a socioeconomic impact from the cost side of the ledger to the benefit side of the ledger will change a cost-benefit ratio but not the measure of net benefits.

With these advantages, NPV is compelling in concept; however, NPV is relatively data-hungry and benefits assessment is sometimes not simple from a method point of view. These disadvantages are apparent when considering socioeconomic impacts. For example, how do we measure and value "equity" in dollar terms? What is the dollar value of doing the right thing?

Costs, Benefits, and Impacts

Cost-benefit evaluation approaches have been critiqued as attempting to shoehorn all relevant decision criteria into a single dollar denominated scalar (net benefits). Costs or benefits that are difficult or expensive to measure are too often omitted: "If it cannot be counted, it does not count.[*] Although this critique has some merit, there is no objective reason why quantitative analysis should preempt a qualitative one. A socioeconomic impact analysis attempts to broaden conventional net benefit analysis, as suggested in Table 6.2.

A socioeconomic analysis broadens the consideration of both costs and benefits and also considers the distributional effects of programs and activities. An analysis of distributional effects considers whether programs make some customers better or worse off, and whether these effects can be mitigated.

Costs and benefits that are difficult or costly to measure can still be identified and qualitatively addressed. The step of identifying all costs and benefits constitutes the first step of good cost-benefit analyses. There also are method resources that have been developed specifically for the application of cost-benefit analyses to water conservation.[†]

---

[*] Some cost-effective methods for assessing cost-effectiveness have been advanced (Pekelney, Chesnutt, and Mitchell 1996a).

[†] The California Urban Water Conservation Council developed two relevant reports: *Guidelines for Preparing Cost-Effectiveness Analyses of Urban Water Conservation BMPs,* September 1996, and *Guide to Data and Methods for Cost-Effectiveness Analyses of Urban Water Conservation Best Management Practices,* July 2000.

Table 6.2

Costs, benefits, and socioeconomic impacts

	Conventional net-benefit analysis	Socioeconomic impact analysis*
Program costs	• Materials • Labor • Rebates or other payments • Marketing and advertising • Administration • Consulting or contracting • Other	• Additional program costs associated with targeting programs to socioeconomic groups • Additional cost of additional rebates or other incentives for targeted programs • Household cost of participation, including indirect costs
Program benefits	• Avoided capital costs • Avoided operating costs	• Improved affordability • Improved bill payment • Avoidance of disconnection • Perceptions of equity • Customer satisfaction • Quality of life • Goodwill
Distributional effects	Generally not considered explicitly	• Effect of program on customer groups based on the distribution of benefits and costs.

*Some costs and benefits can be quantified but not with a high degree of precision.

Pitfalls of these methods are commonly associated with too much attention to a narrow goal without an eye open for unintended consequences that may become apparent in program implementation. For example, lifeline rates might have the unintended consequences of increasing water use among qualifying households with low water use. Rebate programs that are not well targeted may have the unintended consequence of assisting only high-income households and not low-income households. A metering or submetering program may benefit landlords and have adverse effects on low-income renters.

These examples are not presented as foregone conclusions by any means, but, rather, as examples of the type of unintended consequence of which managers need to be aware during program design and implementation. A comprehensive analysis considers benefits, costs, and impacts and potential tradeoffs among competing program goals.

IMPLICATIONS FOR PROGRAM DESIGN

Even a general understanding of costs and benefits, and how they accrue differently for water systems and water customers under alternative programs, can be beneficial for program design and implementation. To illustrate, consider a hypothetical comparison of an untargeted rebate program to a targeted direct-install program. For the untargeted rebate, the utility advertises the rebate at area hardware stores and plumbing supply houses. For the targeted direct-install program, the utility identifies low-income seniors in the service territory and contacts them with the offer of a free toilet replacement. Utility personnel, or contractors working in close collaboration with the utility, perform the replacement.

Table 6.3 identifies the costs and benefits from the water-system and customer perspectives of these two programs. In the case of the untargeted program, a good fraction of the rebate participants may be doing remodels or repairs or otherwise be replacing their toilets. Because the savings from the free-rider customers would occur anyhow, they should not be attributed to the program.

From the water-system perspective, the direct-install program costs include identifying the target audience and completing the installations, where the costs of the rebate program are limited to promotion, the value of the rebate, and installation verification. The benefits to the utility include water savings in both cases; however, for the targeted program, the installations are all for customers who would not replace their toilets otherwise. In other terms, if the targeting is successful, there are few free riders, so the utility can properly attribute all of the water savings to its program. With a targeted program, the utility also achieves a public relations benefit.

Customers participating in the rebate program incur the cost of installation and fixture purchase above the rebate value. The direct-install program involves virtually no costs except for the time to comply with administration and oversee the home installation. The benefits to customers in both programs include water savings and the reduced water bill that results. Again, some of the rebate customers might have accrued these savings even without the program if they would have installed the fixture anyhow. The targeted program will have more direct affordability consequences.

Which of these programs is better? The point of this illustration is to encourage the complete identification of costs and benefits early in program design and to consider more than

Table 6.3
Comparison of costs and benefits to water systems and customers for two programs

	Untargeted rebate	Targeted direct install
Water systems		
Costs	• Promotion and administration • Rebate costs	• Promotion and administration • Cost of fixtures and installation
Benefits	• Water savings (net of savings by free riders) • Avoided system costs associated with water savings	• Water savings from confirmed installation (few free riders to account for) • Avoided system costs associated with water savings • Positive customer relations (target population and generally) • Potential improvement in bill payment by the target population
Water customers		
Costs	• Fixture costs above rebate • Indirect costs associated with participation	• None
Benefits	• Reduction in water bill as a result of water savings • Improved affordability for low-income participating customers • Reduced repair costs • Improvement in fixture quality	• Reduction in water bill as a result of water savings • Improved service affordability for all participating (targeted) customers • Reduced repair costs • Improvement in fixture quality

simply the easily quantified costs and benefits. Similar programs indeed may have different results, as well as socioeconomic impacts.

OBSERVATIONS

As a first step in assessing the socioeconomic impacts of conservation programs, existing policy analysis frameworks and economic methods can be applied. In applying these methods, their inherent shortcomings are not necessarily overcome; nonetheless, they are useful in organizing questions and developing facts and figures. These applications offer several important recommendations. First, they recognize that many of the benefits of programs designed to help the poor, the elderly, or other disadvantaged groups—whether associated with water conservation or other programs and activities—are inherently difficult to quantify. These benefits also are often difficult to value in dollar terms, leading to a systematic underestimation of benefits when net-benefit analysis is employed.

Second, clearly, there are ways to use these analytic tools to learn more about policy decisions, even in the presence of limited data and methods. Using cost-effectiveness analysis or net-benefit analysis as a vehicle for break-even analysis or testing judgmental assumptions can help "bound" the results adequately to provide a defensible foundation for policy action. Finally, using the broader policy analysis framework is often an effective way to organize decision making systematically without relying exclusively on economic or any other single criterion.

CHAPTER 7

APPLICATIONS AND ILLUSTRATIONS

INTRODUCTION

This chapter illustrates ways to apply the framework presented in chapter 6 to examples of conservation planning and evaluation. The objective is to illustrate the salient strengths and weaknesses of the analytic methods, not to develop detailed technically defensible analyses. Five illustrations are provided:

Illustration 1: Cost-Effectiveness Analysis for a Conservation Portfolio

Illustration 2: Research Design for Evaluating a Retrofit Program

Illustration 3: Effect of Conservation on Wastewater Flow

Illustration 4: Predicting Program Participation

Illustration 5: Improved Program Targeting

ILLUSTRATION 1:
COST-EFFECTIVENESS ANALYSIS FOR A CONSERVATION PORTFOLIO

The City of Phoenix Water Services Department serves a population of 1,215,000—approximately 69 percent of the water is used by residential customers. Over the past 15 years, the City has implemented a range of residential-sector conservation programs, including considerable effort to target need-based populations such as low-income families and senior citizens.

Table 7.1 summarizes a subset of these programs. This subset demonstrates the diversity of approaches and levels of targeting intensity. For example, the Low-Income Program targeted customers who qualified for assistance with their water bills. City staff performed a wide range of retrofits and repairs. In contrast, the Target Program was defined by geographic boundaries, not income, and it relied primarily on customer installations, with staff assistance only when needed. The Depot Program relied almost entirely on customers for distribution and installation. The Seniors Program targeted homes with elderly residents, and senior volunteers were paid stipends of $14 per home to conduct the program audits. Some of these homes were referred to a water

Table 7.1

Conservation program characteristics

Program	Description	Devices*	Labor	Cost per intervention†
Low-income	Labor-intensive repair for bill assistance customers	TD, SH, FM, F, A, T	City Staff	$200
Target	Geographically defined, self-install, staff assistance if needed	TD, SH, A	Customer/ Staff	$60
Depot	Customer pick-up and self install	TD, SH, A	Customer	$10
Seniors	Home audits by senior volunteers	TD, SH, A	Volunteers	$30
City-installed	City staff direct installations	TD, SH	City Staff	$150
HSD	Hands-on repairs and upgrades	SH, F, T, FM	Staff/ Contractors	$625
MetroTech	Hands-on repairs and upgrades	SH, F, T, FM	Staff/ Contractors	$625

Source: Data provided by Phoenix Water Services Department.
*TD = toilet device, SH = showerhead, FM = fluidmaster, F = faucets, A = aerators, T = toilets.
†1997 dollars. Costs do not include volunteer or student labor.

conservation officer for major repairs beyond the scope of the volunteers' training level. The City-Installed Program targeted a specific geographic part of the service area—the Union Hills area—for staff-installed retrofits.

The final two programs listed are innovative, collaborative approaches to ULFT installations. The HSD Program was a joint effort with the Human Services Department; the MetroTech Program involved student plumbers from a vocational high school. Both programs provided more extensive repair and replacements. In addition, both programs worked on older, inner-city, ill-maintained buildings that required more time and materials than other programs. Most of the HSD Program was performed by City staff, and most of the MetroTech work was performed by student plumbers with supporting journeyman or retired plumbers who were paid.

The latter two programs were relatively expensive because extensive repairs and materials were necessary to conserve water in the ill-maintained buildings. Since numerous targeted customers were in group homes and homeless shelters, the potential for savings was greater than for typical multifamily residences because of housing density and because older fixtures tend to leak more.

Table 7.2 shows the number of program interventions conducted for each of these diverse programs. Table 7.3 shows the average number of devices installed per program intervention over the life of the program.

Table 7.2

Historical program interventions

Year	Low-income	Target	Depot	Seniors	City-installed	HSD	MetroTech
1985	—	44,000	—	—	—	—	—
1986	—	—	—	—	—	—	—
1987	—	—	—	—	—	—	—
1988	—	—	—	—	—	—	—
1989	171	5,171	781	297	—	—	—
1990	110	9,511	25,733	160	8,501	—	—
1991	27	1,953	8,235	694	98	—	—
1992	17	17	7,534	1,156	2	—	—
1993	15	108	1,440	772	—	—	—
1994	28	1	683	796	—	191	48
1995	13	8,229	309	771	—	82	230
1996	—	29	2	766	—	262	64
1997	—	6	4	109	—	97	34
1998	—	16	7	1	—	73	51
Total	381	69,041	44,728	5,522	8,601	705	427

Source: Data provided by Phoenix Water Services Department.

Table 7.3

Average installed devices per program intervention for all years

	Low-income	Target	Depot	Seniors	City-installed	HSD	MetroTech
Toilet device	1.22	0.89	1.74	0.32	2.04	0.00	—
Showerhead	0.90	0.72	1.19	0.17	1.06	0.15	0.83
Fluidmaster	0.13	0.00	0.00	—	0.00	—	—
Faucets	0.03	0.00	0.00	—	—	0.20	0.43
Aerator	0.11	0.05	0.55	0.05	0.00	—	—
Toilet	0.01	—	0.00	—	—	0.60	0.89

Source: Data provided by Phoenix Water Services Department.
NOTE: Values less than 1 indicate that, on average, less than one device was installed per program intervention.

105

For the purpose of this illustration, we use the assumed savings rates in Table 7.4. This table shows the savings in the first year of the device installation and the assumed decay in savings over a 20-year period. The figures for first-year savings are drawn from empirical studies of conservation programs in several areas of the Southwest. The toilet-savings figure is meant to indicate the savings from typical multifamily residential installations. This may not be applicable to all of the program types. For the programs that targeted seniors, even single-family residences may have use characteristics similar to a typical multifamily residence because retired seniors spend more time at home. Figure 7.1 summarizes total savings over 20 years.

This illustration shows that Phoenix spent money on programs that—at first glance—look costly compared to their avoided cost of water ($63/acre-foot now and up to $300/acre-foot in the

Table 7.4

Savings per device over analysis period

Device year	Toilet device	Showerhead	Fluid master	Faucet	Aerator	Toilet
Year 1 savings in gallons per day	4.0	5.5	4.0	5.5	1.5	48.0
Savings decay per year	50%	10%	10%	10%	50%	2%

Source: Authors' construct using data assembled from a variety of studies in the Southwest.

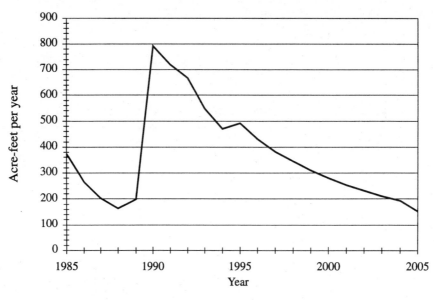

Source: Authors' construct using data described in previous tables.

Figure 7.1   Conservation savings over time

future). It also shows that the cost-effectiveness of the programs varies considerably between programs. What actions are suggested by these results? Is it the standard first-order economic answer: We should line up these conservation programs in order of cost and invest up to the point of avoided water supply? Yes and no. Yes, in that we surely do want conservation programs to invest wisely from an economic perspective. No, in that our economic analysis as it stands is incomplete so we cannot defensibly reach that conclusion.

If the simple conclusion to these results is that none of these programs should be implemented, why were they implemented and why do many consider them worthwhile? A number of reasons have been cited:

- "Benefits accrue to an organizational set larger than just the water utility." This is most apparent in public water agencies that, as part of a government, are also trying to support the health and welfare of its poor and elderly citizens. Although these goals may be stated by the public health and welfare agencies, why should they not be coordinated with other branches of government?

- The programs mitigate the impact of rate increases on the poor and elderly and, thus, facilitate rate changes that are otherwise needed to support water services. Political decision-making bodies, such as the city council, must be responsive to a wide range of community concerns, not just the financial stability of the water department. By helping decision makers respond to their concerns, they can support utility goals.

- Water efficiency is an alternative to rate subsidies, which do not provide strong conservation price signals.

- Reduce the cost of bill collection, disconnection, and arrearages.

These reasons each point to limitations in the simple analysis. A broader analysis would include additional quantified and nonquantified benefits, such as the savings to the welfare agency and the social value of helping those in need. Clearly, a broader set of criteria is needed to assess program impacts, and we need the ability to assess quantitative and qualitative criteria.

For example, consider that on-site retrofits reduce financial burdens on participants and increase the interaction of the City with a group of need-based citizens. We might then consider running the numbers with a different objective in mind—perhaps to find a lower bound to the size of unquantified benefits. One way to do this is to calculate the break-even benefit value per household needed for the program to have benefits at least equal to its costs. The break-even value can be weighed by the decision maker against the social service value. Another way to do this is to work harder at quantifying benefits that can be identified, such as the benefits of reduced bill-collection costs and arrearages.

Yet another approach would be to recognize the joint production costs of the water and social services branches of government and to allocate costs accordingly. For example, if we allocate only part of the program costs—say 50 percent or another appropriate portion—to water conservation, we have a different measure of how program costs compare to the acre-feet of water saved—one that may be more commensurate to the cost of conservation-only programs (those without social welfare joint production). The cost-per-acre-foot results in Table 7.5 would then be one half of their respective values.

To round out this illustration, the perspective of the customer should be considered. Customers in different socioeconomic circumstances have different program experiences. For example, low-income customers (such as those targeted by the HSD and MetroTech programs) may be less likely to benefit from extensive plumbing repairs that have long-term payback periods. Low-income households may have trouble raising and allocating the capital to invest in such repairs. Renters might not be allowed to alter or repair fixtures. The benefits of conservation in terms of cost savings may accrue to the landlord but not necessarily to the tenant in the form of

Table 7.5

Summary of total savings, total costs, and cost per acre-foot

	Low-income	Target	Depot	Seniors	City-installed	HSD	Metro-Tech
Water saved in 2000 (acre-feet/yr)	1.06	88.35	125.39	3.12	19.68	21.87	20.72
Cumulative savings: 1985 to 2025 (acre-foot)	28.9	3,246.4	3,674.6	69.0	650.2	392.2	367.8
Total costs: 1985 to 1998 ($)	76,200	4,142,460	447,282	165,660	1,290,150	440,625	266,875
Cost per acre-foot: 1985 to 2025 ($/acre-foot)	2,146	1,173	97	1,750	1,630	740	480

Source: Authors' construct based on data described in previous tables.

rent reductions. The residency of some low-income persons may be more transient—they may simply move more frequently to pursue job opportunities or seek better or more affordable housing. For customers in these circumstances, a long payback period may be unattractive or unacceptable and a barrier to program participation.

In quantitative terms, payback period is the time it takes for the sum of benefits to exceed the sum of costs. In more formal terms, accounting for the time value of money, the payback period is the time it takes discounted benefits to meet or exceed discounted costs. An HSD Program household, for example, that received a toilet, faucet, and showerhead replacement would save approximately 59 gallons per day when first implemented, according to the savings figures in Table 7.4. Even if the savings decay rate is ignored, savings per year would be about $29 per year with a commodity charge of $1/ccf. As seen in Table 7.6, the payback is more than 13 years, even if the customer faces only one half of the $625 program costs. For many low-income or fixed-income customers, even a subsidized initial outlay may be prohibitive.

Indeed, customer payback periods can be used to help program managers understand the special perspectives of low-income or fixed-income customers. This can provide the manager with additional insight that can help focus programs and improve effectiveness. These methods also can be used to develop the distributional analysis needed to assess differences in program impacts among socioeconomic groups within the utility's service area.

ILLUSTRATION 2:
RESEARCH DESIGN FOR EVALUATING A RETROFIT PROGRAM

To expand on Illustration 1, Illustration 2 delves further into the issue of research design and evaluation. How does one apply research methods to determine conservation savings from programs targeted at need-based populations? For example, the direct plumbing retrofit program (introduced earlier) was performed by students from a local vocational high school (MetroTech). This program was geographically targeted and required no income testing for eligibility.

A fundamental approach to evaluating this program is "intervention analysis" using utility billing histories. In its simplest form, an intervention analysis (Box and Tiao 1975) would measure the change in water use resulting from participation in this conservation program.

Table 7.6

Illustration of customer payback from investment in conservation

Year	Savings	Discounted savings	Cumulative net benefits
0	—	—	$(312.50)
1	$28.86	$28.02	(284.48)
2	28.86	27.20	(257.28)
3	28.86	26.41	(230.88)
4	28.86	25.64	(205.24)
5	28.86	24.89	(180.34)
6	28.86	24.17	(156.18)
7	28.86	23.46	(132.71)
8	28.86	22.78	(109.93)
9	28.86	22.12	(87.82)
10	28.86	21.47	(66.34)
11	28.86	20.85	(45.50)
12	28.86	20.24	(25.26)
13	28.86	19.65	(5.61)
14	28.86	19.08	13.47
15	28.86	18.52	31.99
16	28.86	17.98	49.97
17	28.86	17.46	67.43
18	28.86	16.95	84.38
19	28.86	16.46	100.84
20	28.86	15.98	116.82

Source: Authors' construct. Assumes the customer invests one half of the initial $625 investment.

Consider Equation 7.1. The variable on the left side is water consumption derived from the utility billing histories. It is easier to form a consistent basis for comparison if the billed consumption variable is converted to an average daily water use. To this measure of water use, one must match a measure of the "intervention" program participation (yes equals one, no equals zero), device count, or index of participation intensity. To illustrate, a simple "intervention analysis" model can be estimated for multiple-family installations where the intervention is ULFT installation. The form of the model would be:

$$Use = \mu_i + \beta_T \cdot T + \beta_{Units} \cdot Units + \varepsilon \tag{7.1}$$

where *Use* = water consumption (in gallons per day per meter)

    T = the count of ULFTs replaced

    Units = the number of dwelling units in the complex

    ε = the equation error

The parameter μ_i represents mean water consumption per meter i. The parameter β_T represents the effect of installing an ULFT and is expected to be negative (installing a ULFT reduces water consumption). The parameter β_{Units} represents the effect of additional dwelling units associated with a meter and is expected to be positive (more dwelling units means more water consumption). The parameter ε represents the "error term" of the equation—everything else left unexplained by the systematic portion of the model. The volume of water savings is then derived by multiplying the estimated mean water savings per toilet (β_T) times the number of toilets: Total Expected Savings = ($\beta_T \cdot T$).

This model could be used to measure the net water savings directly attributable to this program through construction of an appropriate (matching) control group. The net water savings would then be the difference between water savings in the participant and control groups. Program implementation start, for example, with a subset of a target population, using another matched group as controls. In this first phase, program savings could be estimated and program implementation strategies could be refined.

The model could also test for the preprogram differences between participants and other utility customers. Were participants using more water than other nonparticipating customers, given observed characteristics? This, in turn, can inform future program targeting. Finally, the model can be used to identify characteristics of households that achieved higher water savings. This too can inform program targeting.

Of course, real-world application of this type of research design must also address numerous practical difficulties: data validation, appropriate transformation of the left-hand-side variable, testing for individual households that greatly change the results, and communicating the results of the analysis in ways useful to decision makers.[*] However, the investment in carefully

---

[*] Additional pointers for conducting an effective impact evaluation can be found in Pekelney, Chesnutt, and Hanemann 1996.

111

conducted research has the potential to yield benefits in terms of program effectiveness and cost effectiveness, as well as program documentation and accountability.

It should be noted that when a program is designed to achieve goals other than simply saving water (community affairs, customer outreach, and affordability concerns), the estimated water savings might be less important for program justification than for integration into ongoing utility planning. Again, we stress that costs and savings results must be interpreted in the context of the broader policy-decision framework, as described in chapter 6.

ILLUSTRATION 3:
EFFECT OF CONSERVATION ON WASTEWATER FLOW

Water conservation also reduces wastewater flows. In fact, wastewater capacity savings can be one of the major desirable benefits for many (indoor) conservation programs. To the extent that program managers can identify the range of wastewater benefits, the remaining unquantified "social value" benefits, often difficult to document, can be accounted for by qualitative methods only.

For example, ULFT water savings can reasonably be expected to correspond to wastewater-flow reduction. If the full range of wastewater benefits was incorporated in the Phoenix example described in Illustration 1, we would see more positive conclusions in terms of cost effectiveness.

One complication that does need to be addressed is the expected change in concentration of the wastewater flow. It is relatively straightforward to derive the percentage change in wastewater concentration that results from a percentage change in interior water use/flow (Equation 7.2).

$$Concentration = \frac{Mass}{Volume}$$

or

$$C = \frac{M}{V} \tag{7.2}$$

Given $V' \equiv V \cdot (1 + \%\Delta V)$, find $\%\Delta C$.

$$\%\Delta C \equiv \frac{\dfrac{M}{V} - \dfrac{M}{V'}}{\dfrac{M}{V}} = 1 - \frac{\dfrac{M}{V'}}{\dfrac{M}{V}} = 1 - \frac{\dfrac{1}{V \cdot (1 + \%\Delta V)}}{\dfrac{1}{V}} = 1 - \frac{1}{1 + \%\Delta V} \qquad (7.3)$$

Documenting the effects on wastewater flow is important for several reasons. First, the benefits of conservation on the wastewater side are often expressed as avoided costs. These benefits can be realized only if, in fact, these wastewater-capacity costs are avoided. Thus, the effects of conservation must be incorporated into utility planning for conservation to have its intended benefit. Cost-effective conservation plays an integral role in integrated resource planning.

The act of documenting a potential benefit from avoidable wastewater system costs can make the case for cost sharing of conservation programs between water and wastewater utilities. Many wastewater systems are facing daunting challenges of maintaining aging facilities and expanding to meet demand growth. With such large capital investments at stake and with the rate impacts they imply, managers welcome ways to defer, downsize, or eliminate capital investments.

Even if cost-sharing or beneficial effects of conservation for wastewater system planning are ignored, wastewater engineers and planners can take advantage of identified and predictable changes in the physical makeup of future waste streams. Maintenance and expansion efforts, for example, can focus on concentration rather than volume. This is particularly important when determining design capacity that is based on stormwater flows.

A final consideration is especially important from a socioeconomic-impact perspective. Customers paying a volumetric rate for wastewater services realize an additional benefit on their bill. The positive bill impact of water-use reductions on low-income households is therefore magnified. In analytical terms, a more comprehensive scope of benefits can be quantified by considering the joint effects of conservation on water and wastewater costs and prices. The combined billing effect is related directly to the affordability of water and wastewater services, and therefore has much relevance in the context of socioeconomic impact analysis.[*]

---

[*] Pricing effects are explored further in chapter 8.

ILLUSTRATION 4:
PREDICTING PROGRAM PARTICIPATION

This example is based on an impact evaluation performed for the Los Angeles Department of Water and Power,[*] another study participant. In this illustration, a model was developed to predict the probability of installing a device from a retrofit kit that was hung on the doorknob during a drought emergency. A key question was whether the probability of installation was improved by door-to-door follow-up visits. The raw descriptive statistics were not encouraging: the participant group with no follow-up had a 50 percent probability of installing a low-flow showerhead or a toilet dam. Alternatively, the groups that had follow-up visits had a 44 percent probability of installation. These participant groups were known to have had very different socioeconomic characteristics, and a statistical modeling effort was needed to account for these differences.

The study estimated a model for the probability of installation using standard discrete-choice methods (a logistic regression). The model found that the likelihood of installation was lower for homes with more residents working full-time outside the home; homes with a pool; and larger, newer homes. Clearly, many of these characteristics are positively correlated with income. By controlling for socioeconomic differences among the groups, the study found a positive effect of follow-up on the probability of installation.

This illustration shows the importance of incorporating household characteristics in the evaluation of conservation programs. Conclusions based on the raw descriptive statistics would be incorrect and would lead to the conclusion that follow-up had no impact on compliance rates. The modeling effort quantifies the effect of follow-up and allows evaluation of the cost effectiveness of adding follow-up to conservation programs. It further allows managers of low-income programs to better understand their target audience and program impact.

---

[*] See Metropolitan Water District of Southern California and the Los Angeles Department of Water and Power 1991, Appendix C.

114

ILLUSTRATION 5:
IMPROVED PROGRAM TARGETING

As the information technology and data available to water utilities continue to improve, there will be additional opportunities to harness available information to improve targeting of conservation programs. As an example, residential water surveys have often been targeted by sending solicitation letters to high water users. This method is both simple—based on a straightforward sort of water consumption billing histories—and an improvement over an untargeted program. Many agencies are reexamining this targeting rule, looking for a better estimate of water-savings potential. If this type of customer outreach can be better targeted to where it does the most good, the cost effectiveness of residential surveys can be improved.

Several municipalities have made progress in integrating other data sources with their water-system data. Examples include census data, assessor tax data, and imaging data. One proposal for improving the targeting rule used data on lot size and home size to construct a rough but consistent estimate of water-use efficiency—inches of water applied per square foot of irrigable area. This second targeting rule has been used and it successfully identified households having inefficient water practices. It can also find inefficient homes having small yards and, hence, small conservation potential. Other targeting rules can be created to develop more fully the targeting rule into a measure of conservation potential. These program-targeting rules are presented in Table 7.7 (with additional derivation detail provided in Table 7.8).

These conservation-targeting rules provide the logic for a set of targeting rules tailored to low-income programs or other programs where socioeconomic impacts are important:

- Total water use can be used as a screening criterion. However, since low-income households are often living in multifamily dwellings, at least in urban areas, adjustments can be made for persons per household rather than irrigable area.

- In rural areas, irrigable area could be delineated further into categories of aesthetic landscape and food-producing landscape. Although water-use efficiency is a goal for all end uses, the financial impacts can be considered in the broader household financial picture, including food costs.

115

Table 7.7

Residential survey program targeting rules

Total Use

    Rule 1:   Annual Water Use

Peak-Use Efficiency

    Rule 2:   (July Use – Jan Use) / Irr_area

Total Savings

    Rule 3:   Irr_area * { [(Annual_Use – Constant Allowance) / Irr_area] – ETo Allowance}

Seasonal Variant of Total Savings

    Rule 4:   a * Irr_area {[(July_Use – Constant Allowance) / Irr_area] – ETo Allowance} +
                (1- a) * Irr_area {[(Jan_Use – Constant Allowance) / Irr_area] – ETo Allowance}

Definitions

Annual Water Use (HCF) – This measure of water consumption is improved by standardizing for the number of days. (Some accounts may have missing reads.)

July–Aug Water Use (HCF) – Highest consumption read

Jan–Feb Water Use (HCF) – Lowest consumption read

Estimated Irrigable area (ft^2)
    Irrigable_area = Lot Size (ft^2) – HouseArea (ft^2) / Stories – 360 (ft^2) * pool – 240 (ft^2) *
    OneCarGarage – 400 (ft^2) * TwoCarGarage – .20 * LotSize(ft^2)

Estimated Irrigated turf area (ft^2)
    Irr_area = Irrigable_area * 0.5

Allowance = Constant Allowance + ETo Allowance
    Constant Allowance = 70 gpd * Persons/HH + 40 gpd * Pool
    ETo Allowance = .8 * (Evapotranspiration –.4 * Precipitation)

The parameter a is a fraction between zero and one to weight the summer and winter indices.

Source: Authors' construct. Estimated irrigable area from Thomas Pape, Best Management Partners.

Table 7.8

Derivation of targeting residential surveys by total potential water savings

Rule 3 combines two previously used rules:

Total_Savings = Total_Use * Potential_change_in_efficiency

The industry standard uses the first part of this equation as a targeting rule (Rule 1). This would be the perfect rule if the potential for changing efficiency were absolutely constant across households. Then higher observed consumption would imply higher total potential water savings.

Targeting Rule 2 calculates an estimate of the second part of this equation, efficiency. Efficiency minus a constant (an allowance) gives the estimate of the change in efficiency. Specifically, on the assumption that winter consumption was largely indoor end uses, the January-February consumption was subtracted from July-August consumption prior to dividing by the estimate of irrigated area.

(July Use – Jan Use) / Irr_area)   (Rule 2)

This is the perfect rule when January consumption is composed entirely of indoor end uses and households tend to exhibit similar levels of water consumption. Then higher values of Rule 3 would imply greater inefficiency and total potential water savings.

The Total Savings Rule 3 combines these two types of rules. (Rule 4 is a seasonal version of Rule 3.) First, we find the measure of annual household water consumption:

EQ1:   Annual_Water_Use (gpd)

Second a constant allowance is subtracted from annual water consumption:

EQ2:   Annual_Use – Constant Allowance = EQ1 – 70 gpd * Persons/HH + 40 gpd * Pool

Third, this volume of water is converted from three dimensions into two dimensions by dividing by area:

EQ3:   Annual_Use – Constant Allowance/Irr_area = EQ2 / Irr_area = Applied water in inches per sq ft

Fourth, a basic allowance is made for the evapotranspiration requirements of landscape.

EQ4:   [(Annual_Use – Constant Allowance) / Irr_area] – ETo Allowance = Q3 – .8 *(ETo-.4*Rainfall)

The 80 percent of evapotranspiration requirements has been used historically as a cut off among landscape professionals. Homes using less than 80 percent of evapotranspiration requirements would probably not benefit from a residential survey. The 40 percent effective rainfall parameter comes from two empirical studies. Water use above the allowable ETo allowance (EQ4) is presumed to be potential water savings. The last step is to convert the two-dimensional measure of potential savings back into volumetric terms.

EQ5:
Irr_area X {[(Annual_Use – Constant Allowance) / Irr_area] – ETo Allowance}   (Rule 3)

Source: Authors' construct. See also Bamezai 1997 and Pekelney, Chesnutt, and Hanemann 1996.

- Landscape in urban areas may be managed by landlords rather than tenants, and programs that target apartment buildings may have indirect impacts if savings can be passed on to the tenants.

Actual application of these targeting rules requires field tests to determine which estimates of water-savings potential can, in fact, be realized. Homes having higher conservation potential will realize no water savings if they do not participate. Nonetheless, targeting of residential survey programs can be expected to lead to increased efforts to develop better methods as a way to increase water savings and improve net benefits.

OPPORTUNITIES

The illustrations presented above show the different ways in which existing analytic methods can be brought to bear on questions of the socioeconomic impacts of conservation. Perhaps the most important conclusions to draw from these illustrations are that (1) the information that decision makers have is contingent upon their support of analytic efforts that examine socioeconomic characteristics and (2) the objectives of such studies can be focused on questions concerning the socioeconomic impacts of conservation programs and the influence of socioeconomic characteristics on the effectiveness of all residential conservation programs more generally. In sum, the conceptual approach in chapter 2 has been illustrated in concrete terms.

CHAPTER 8

SOCIOECONOMIC EVALUATION OF WATER PRICING

INTRODUCTION

Water pricing in general, and pricing for conservation purposes, raises a number of challenging issues with regard to benefits, costs, and socioeconomic impacts. Accurate price signals are needed to achieve economic efficiency in production and consumption decisions. Prices that are too low can encourage too much consumption, thereby undermining conservation goals. Therefore, pricing can be considered a necessary, but often insufficient, component of a conservation strategy.

The concept of cost-based rates* sounds simple enough. However, these methods have implications both for affordability and for conservation. Conservation-oriented pricing tends to emphasize the basic principles of cost-of-service pricing; that is, prices should reflect the cost of service in general and the cost of serving different groups of customers or providing different types of services. Alternative methods for allocating costs, however, can result in very different customer impacts. Conservation-oriented pricing can present a challenge in terms of distributional impacts.

As noted in chapter 4, price has very direct and potentially significant impacts on one socioeconomic factor in particular: income. Other things being equal, an increase in prices, which may be necessary to achieve efficiency goals, will consume more of a household's financial resources. Customers that can conserve and thereby adjust their total water usage downward may be positioned to keep their water bill constant. Customers that choose not to conserve, or those who cannot conserve, will see an increase in their water bills. Water service will take a greater share of the household budget. For low-income or fixed-income customers, a consequence is that the household must sacrifice other purchases in order to pay the water bill. A more serious potential consequence is nonpayment. In the extreme, high utility bills have been regarded as a contributing factor to homelessness (Saunders 1992).

---

* The term "cost-based rates" is used here generally to mean rates that reflect the "true" cost of service (including practical applications of marginal-cost pricing) in order to promote efficient water use and conservation.

Even utilities without conservation programs should consider the effect of price changes on water usage and on customers. This chapter provides an overview and illustration of tools for evaluating the effect of general and conservation-oriented price changes on water demand, utility revenues, and customers. All three have socioeconomic dimensions. Particular attention is paid to the evaluation of customer impacts.

RATE DESIGN AS A CONSERVATION PROGRAM

Rate design is a core utility function. All water utilities must set rates in order to recover revenue requirements from customers. In many respects, rate design also serves as a type of conservation program. An increase in rates, as well as other changes in rate design, can encourage or discourage conservation behavior. Utilities also can use pricing in conjunction with education, rebates, and other conservation programs to induce changes in water consumption behavior. Pricing also can be used during droughts and other water-supply emergencies to communicate scarcity.

Conservation Rates

No clear consensus exists about what constitutes a conservation-oriented water rate. Because conservation can be defined as a beneficial reduction in water use (Baumann, Boland, and Hanemann 1998), a conservation rate can be defined as one that helps accomplish this goal. In the realm of policy analysis, a beneficial solution is one that yields positive benefits relative to costs. As previously discussed, benefits and costs ideally are assessed at the societal level, but other perspectives—such as that of the utility—can be assessed as well.

Conservation pricing, or any volumetric pricing, for that matter, requires metering. A simple, uniform rate (one in which the amount charged per unit of consumption is constant) can be considered conservation oriented because the amount of a customer's water bill rises with consumption. A change from a decreasing-block to a uniform rate, therefore, is considered a shift in the direction of conservation pricing.

Other rates structures considered conservation oriented are seasonal rates, increasing-block rates, water-needs-based rates, indoor–outdoor rates, and excess-use rates. Each of theses rates attempts to fine-tune the rate signal according to perceptions about how efficiency can best be achieved. Evaluating their effectiveness is beyond the scope of this report; however, a number of resources are available for this purpose (Chesnutt et al. 1996). As discussed in later sections, however, even subtle changes in the rate structure can have different socioeconomic impacts.

Implementation

From a programmatic perspective, a change in pricing can be relatively straightforward to implement. In fact, pricing strategies can be highly cost effective to the extent that implementation costs are relatively low. The most significant costs associated with changing the rate design come from the cost-of-service study and from any necessary changes in billing and metering practices.

The cost-of-service study is used to evaluate and allocate the cost of providing service to different customer groups. A cost-of-service study that also includes an assessment of customer impacts on billing changes may require more resources than a traditional study, but the investment may be worthwhile to a utility that wants to be better informed about these effects.

Changes to billing and metering may be more costly. Monthly metering and billing generally is needed when utilities want to use seasonal rates or other rate variations designed to differentiate rates for indoor usage. A change from quarterly to monthly billing may require software (and possibly hardware) changes. Postage costs will approximately triple. Additional costs also are incurred if the utility shifts from a postcard to an envelope-style bill format. Other administrative costs might also be incurred in terms of additional staff and other resources.

The cost of implementing a rate design change can be summarized as follows:

Cost of rate design change $= f$ (cost-of-service study, hardware and software, metering and billing, other administrative costs)

Generally, these costs compare favorably to other types of conservation programs. To evaluate the economic efficiency of the pricing program, these costs should be compared to the benefits achieved in terms of water savings.

Concerns about socioeconomic impacts, however, add another dimension to the analysis. Different rate design options will tend to have different benefits, as well as different effects on customers. An additional analysis of these effects can help utility managers to decide among rate options in terms of how customers are affected and to design programs that mitigate adverse consequences of some types of rate changes.

Table 8.1 provides an example of rate design changes that water utilities might implement for conservation purposes.

EVALUATING IMPACTS OF RATE DESIGN

Numerous evaluation methods are available to predict the impact of conservation rate structures on water demand, utility revenues, and customers (Chesnutt et al. 1996). These same methods or "tools" can be focused to gain greater understanding of questions related to socioeconomic characteristics and socioeconomic outcomes. First, how do socioeconomic characteristics

Table 8.1

Sample rate changes

Type of rate	$ per ccf
Uniform rate	$2.05
Uniform seasonal rate	
Winter	$1.34
Summer	$2.98
Increasing-block rate	
First block	$1.99
Second block	$2.38
Usage level for tier breakpoint	45 ccf
Seasonal increasing-block rate	
First block	$1.95
Winter—second block	$2.33
Usage level for tier breakpoint	40 ccf
Summer—second block	$2.98
Usage level for tier breakpoint	50 ccf

help us understand the impact of conservation rate structures on water demand and utility revenues? Second, what is the impact of conservation rate structures on socioeconomic outcomes?

Three established methods for evaluating rate impacts on water utilities and customers also are reviewed:

1. Demand analysis is used to evaluate the effect of rate alternatives on water demand.
2. Revenue analysis is used to evaluate the effect of rate alternatives on agency revenue and finances.
3. Customer-impact analysis is used to evaluate the effect of rate alternatives on customer bills.

Of course, these are not the only tools available to understand the broad range of socioeconomic impacts. Instead, these methods are only meant to illustrate the potential payoff from applying several common empirical tools to socioeconomic issues. Socioeconomic effects can certainly involve important indirect or difficult-to-quantify impacts that may also need to be included for a comprehensive and useful understanding.

Water conservation programs can include rebates for water-efficient devices, education, on-site review or retrofit, and other activities, all of which may be used with or without a coordinated conservation-oriented rate structure. Nonetheless, all rate structures provide incentives that influence water use, whether by design or by coincidence. Predicting the response to utility-sponsored conservation programs and their impacts requires inclusion of utility rates and their incentive effects.

DEMAND ANALYSIS

Demand analysis forms the foundation of utility revenue analysis and customer-impact analysis. By understanding what drives demand in a service territory, including socioeconomic factors, utilities will be better able to predict and shape future demand patterns. Moreover, a demand analysis can help utilities understand and respond to the needs of different service populations within their territories.

Demand analysis is essential for understanding the potential effects of a change in rates on water usage by customers. As introduced in chapter 3, aggregate water demand is a function of a variety of factors, including climate, price, and socioeconomic characteristics of the service territory. Household water use, a more precise measurement, is influenced by these factors as well (measured at the household level). Analysts need to know how rate structures influence individual aggregate demand and consumptive choices for water services before the impacts on utility revenues and customer bills can be reliably understood or predicted.

The level and shape of future water demand directly affects the sizing of future water and wastewater treatment capacity and, thereby, the benefit of avoided capacity through demand management. Sound demand management requires an understanding of rate impacts on water demand and future capacity requirements. Factors usually cited as causes of fluctuations and trend changes in water demand include price, population growth, economic growth, climate, and weather. In addition to these factors, socioeconomic conditions and characteristics of the population influence water demand. Is population growth occurring in suburbs with large irrigated lots or in urban high-rises? Is population density growing in areas that are economically strapped? Are income, age, or other characteristics of a service area changing?

REVENUE ANALYSIS

When conducting financial and revenue analysis of conservation rate structures, at least two important methods exist in which socioeconomic characteristics are important. First, as we discussed above, socioeconomic characteristics are important when forecasting water demand, at both the system level and the household level. Forecasting system demand is an essential foundation for revenue forecasts; with block rates, the distribution of forecast demand is also essential. Second, socioeconomic characteristics are important determinants of bill-payment behavior (including delinquency).

Use Distribution and Sales Forecasts

Conservation rate structures, like other rate structures, are designed to achieve future revenue requirements. A simple model of future sales drives many financial analyses. For example, sales next year will be like sales last year. Alternatively, the trend in sales will equal the trend in the preceding 10 years. Though these methods are simple, they do not account explicitly for the effects of climate and weather, the effects of water rates, or the effects of socioeconomic characteristics in the service area.

Incorporating the response of demand to price, especially block prices, is an important improvement on financial analyses. Often, a simple correction in demand estimates is made by multiplying the scheduled change in price by price elasticity to produce a predicted change in use. For example, a 10-percent increase in price would yield a 1-percent decrease in demand with a price elasticity of −0.1. The change in price should be expressed in inflation-adjusted real terms. Recovery of wastewater costs through a commodity charge on water use adds an additional price to water consumption that needs to be incorporated into the measure of price i.

Revenue prediction for rate design requires a short-run price elasticity estimate that reflects the demand response possible within a 1- or 2-year period. Most published empirical literature on price elasticity focuses on long-run estimates. In rate design, do not make the mistake of using long-run response estimates developed for planning purposes. Agencies concerned about uncertainty surrounding the price elasticity should conduct sensitivity analyses to see how much predicted revenue will change with different price-elasticity assumptions.

The method of predicting demand response to rate changes provided thus far affects average water demand. Block-rate structures, however, require more than a model of average (mean) water demand. Revenue prediction requires a model of the entire demand distribution (Chesnutt et al. 1995).

Illustration of Revenue Analysis

Customer billing records can be used to depict demand distributions. The distribution of customer use tends to be skewed. To illustrate, let's say a random sample of single-family customers was taken from a hypothetical agency. The histogram is presented in Figure 8.1. For the purposes of illustration, Figure 8.1 depicts a hypothetical demand distribution with values for the mean and standard deviation (logarithm of bimonthly use) of 3.4 and 0.7, respectively. The distribution is notably skewed; relatively few customers use a large amount of water.

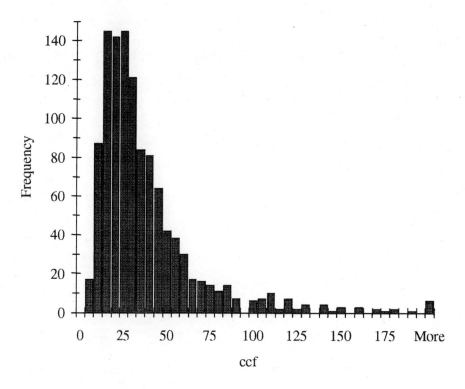

Figure 8.1　Annual distribution of water use

A right-skewed distribution characterizes water use in most water agencies and complicates the design of block-rate structures. Suppose an agency wants to design an increasing-block rate structure with two blocks. It directly follows in Figure 8.2 that if the switch point—where the first block ends and the second begins—were set to median water use (about 31 ccf), half of the customers would see the lower price in the first block and half of the customers would face the higher price in block 2. Does this mean half of all water consumption is facing price 1 and the other half is facing price 2? Because each customer facing the block 1 price uses less water than any customer facing the block 2 price, the water consumed by the customer facing the block 1 price will comprise less than half of total consumption.

Figure 8.2 plots the proportion of customer accounts falling into the second block as the block switch point changes. To estimate revenue, the analyst must know how much water is affected by the higher price in the second block. Figure 8.2 also illustrates that the proportion of total water usage (combined block 1 and block 2 usage) by accounts that have at least some upper-block use is greater than the proportion of accounts that have at least some upper-block use. This fact is directly implied by the right-skewed distribution of water consumption.

126

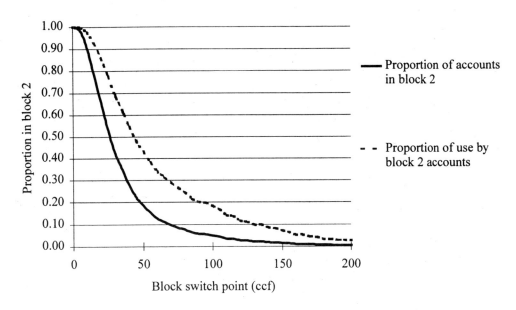

Figure 8.2   Customer accounts compared to water use in an upper block

The propensity of a rate structure to generate revenues that exactly match the revenue requirements of a water agency is subject to risks involving both supply and demand. These risks can produce revenue instability in the form of both revenue surpluses and revenue shortfalls. These risks are associated with changes in the number of customers, changes in customer mix (for example, the loss of a large user), changes in usage patterns, changes in weather, changes in conservation ethic, changes in the price elasticity of water demands, and changes in rate structure (Beecher and Mann 1990).

Among the sources of demand risk and uncertainty are socioeconomic characteristics of the service-area population. Changes in population age, housing density, income, and other factors will alter the distribution of water use. Water-use distributions used for revenue forecasting have to be, at least, tested for sensitivity to assumptions of future trends in socioeconomic characteristics. For example, a service area that is undergoing rapid commercial development may be seeing a decrease in irrigated landscape and an increase in parking lots. As the distribution of income changes over time as the result of the growing globalization of the world economy, low-income housing may become more densely populated and high-income areas may become more intensely irrigated.

These analyses can be used to assess the overall effect of rate-structure changes in terms of changes in water bills across the utility's customer accounts. As seen in Figure 8.3, a revenue-neutral rate-design change will cause some accounts to reflect bill decreases, while others reflect increases.

127

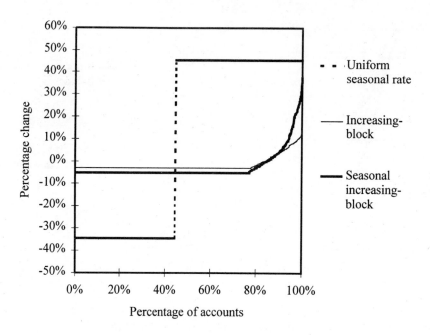

Figure 8.3   Rate changes and relative change in water bills for customer accounts

Bill-Payment Delinquency

In low-income populations and during times of economic downturn, the rate of delinquent bill-paying is higher. This affects revenues and revenue requirements because greater administrative costs are required to manage the delinquent payments, including tracking and noticing late bills and managing time-payment programs. In addition, costs may be incurred because of delayed revenue streams and bill-forgiveness programs.

CUSTOMER-IMPACT ANALYSIS

Changes in rates and rate structure, even revenue-neutral changes, can impact socioeconomic outcomes. The rate analyst can (1) calculate the change in customer bills that would result from a change in rates, (2) identify subgroups that have relatively larger bill impacts, (3) inform the rate-making process about those impacts, and (4) investigate measures to mitigate adverse impacts on specific customer groups. Avoiding unintentional rate shock is an important role that rate evaluation can play. Examples of relevant bill-impact categories include

- Annual change in customer bills for water and wastewater service
- Average change in peak-period (usually summer) bills
- Average change in bills among customers with different seasonal water-use patterns
- Change in bills among small, medium, and large customers in each customer class
- Average impact by voting district or other geopolitical boundaries
- Change in bills for customer groups that have been vocal in previous rate-setting processes

The importance of a careful and thorough bill-impact analysis is difficult to overstate. The bottom line for the public and most decision makers is the impact that water rate structures have on customer bills. If the bill structure has a disproportionate impact on low-income populations with high housing density or on high-income populations with large landscapes, the impacts will be felt and may come back to haunt decision makers. Bill-impact analyses are worthy of significant investment in rate-evaluation resources. Several illustrations are provided.

Illustrations of Customer-Impact Analysis

Metering

When utilities introduce metering and billing, customers are affected. In fact, metering alone is understood to produce significant conservation effects.[*] When utilities move from a flat rate to a metered rate, the impact on customers should be assessed. If the cost of the meters and their installation is imposed directly on customers, affordability may be an issue. Additional administrative costs associated with metering also will affect rates for service.

These concerns also hold for the introduction of submetering to multifamily housing. Customers that have never paid for water service directly will be affected in terms of having a new utility bill that will take a share of the monthly budget. The new obligation may or may not be offset by reductions in rent. If not, submetering can have a distributional effect that favors landlords over

---

[*] These effects can be measured by the "metering elasticity of demand."

renters. Some methods of submetering involve added administrative fees or charges.[*] Utilities must be aware that the transition to making direct payments for water service may be difficult for some customers. An understandable rate structure, along with communication and customer service, can help mitigate adverse effects. Some utilities may want to establish special-assistance programs funded through grants, customer contributions, or other revenue sources.

Similarly, connection fees and system-development fees also have socioeconomic impacts that should be evaluated. For high-income developments, fees can be used to extract a significant source of financial capital for the utility. In effect, fees affect the pattern and pace of development. For low-income developments, high fees can be highly deleterious if they have the effect of pricing housing out of reach.

Fees can be pegged to anticipated water use and socioeconomic factors, which tend to be correlated. Higher fees may be appropriate for higher-income areas that can afford the fees and are likely to see higher water use. The effects of alternative fee options on customers can be evaluated by comparing charges to income levels in the service territory.

Billing Cycle

A change to monthly billing (illustrated in Table 8.2) can be used to sharpen the price signal and is essential for an effective seasonal rate structure. Monthly billing also can have a positive impact on low-income and fixed-income households. Monthly billing does not actually lower total customer water bills. In fact, the additional administrative costs associated with monthly billing might cause a slight increase in bills.

From the customer's viewpoint, however, a monthly bill will be smaller in magnitude than a quarterly bill and may be easier to pay. A monthly bill probably will be more predictable from a budgeting standpoint. Also, by shortening the time period between consumptive actions and cost consequences, the monthly bill can encourage the customer to implement conservation measures that will help keep water service affordable. In other words, the change in the billing cycle may have a conservation effect on water consumption.

---

[*] Such charges also raise legal and regulatory considerations, in additional to financial impact concerns.

Table 8.2

Illustrated impact of billing-cycle change

	Quarterly bill	Monthly bill
Water usage	15,000 gallons	5,000 gallons
Variable charge (@ $2.50/1,000 gallons)	$37.50	$12.50
Comparison with additional administrative costs in monthly bill		
Water usage	15,000 gallons	5,000 gallons
Variable charge (@ $2.65/1,000 gallons for monthly bill)	$37.50	$13.25
Comparison with additional administrative costs in monthly bill and 3 percent reduction in usage		
Water usage	15,000 gallons	4,850 gallons
Variable charge (@ $2.65/1,000 gallons for monthly bill)	$37.50	$12.85

NOTE: Metering unit constraints are ignored in this example.

The water utility can evaluate customer payment before and after introducing monthly billing to look for reductions in nonpayment or late payments.

Rate Levels

As discussed in chapters 3 and 4, differences in socioeconomic circumstances and responsiveness to price (elasticity) mean that changes in rates will have different impacts on different types of customers. Estimates of price and income elasticity can be used to evaluate the effect of rate changes. The illustrations provided here focus only on hypothetical water charges. However, analysts should consider the combined effects of water and wastewater charges for a more complete understanding of socioeconomic impacts.

Although the income correlation for urban–suburban customers is imperfect, the dichotomy can be used to illustrate these effects. Table 8.3 illustrates the distributional implications of rate increases based on differences in price elasticity between a hypothetical urban/multifamily housing customer and a suburban/single-family housing customer. Simple illustrative price elasticity estimates are used: –.05 for the urban customer and –.10 for the suburban customer (reflecting more discretionary water usage).

Table 8.3

Illustrated impact of rate-structure change: 10, 20, and 40 percent variable charge increases

	Multifamily or urban household	Single-family or suburban household
Monthly water use before rate increase	5,000 gallons	6,500 gallons
Current water bill: Variable charge (@ $2.50/1,000 gallons)	$12.50	$16.25
Simplified composite price elasticity of demand (summer and winter)	–0.05	–0.10
10-percent rate increase		
Monthly water after rate increase	4,975 gallons	6,435 gallons
Revised bill following a 10 percent rate increase in the variable charge: Variable charge (@ $2.75/1,000 gallons)	$13.68	$17.70
Percentage increase in total water bill	9.45 percent	8.90 percent
20-percent rate increase		
Monthly water after rate increase	4,950 gallons	6,370 gallons
Revised bill following a 20 percent rate increase in the variable charge: Variable charge (@ $3.00/1,000 gallons)	$14.85	$19.11
Percentage increase in total water bill	18.80 percent	17.60 percent
40-percent rate increase		
Monthly water after rate increase	4,900 gallons	6,240 gallons
Revised bill following a 40 percent rate increase in the variable charge: Variable charge (@ $3.50/1,000 gallons)	$17.15	$21.84
Percentage increase in total water bill	37.20 percent	34.40 percent

NOTE: These illustrations do not include fixed charges. Metering unit constraints are ignored.

Rate Structures

A relatively popular concept in conservation pricing is to fine-tune the rate so prices are higher for customers driving more costly peak demand. Several variations in peak-demand pricing can be identified:

- Seasonal rates that charge a higher unit price during the peak season of water use (usually the summer)

- Indoor/outdoor rates that charge a higher unit price for outdoor use, sometimes based on an analysis of off-peak usage patterns
- Excess-use rates that establish a base level of usage and price usage in excess of this threshold at a higher unit price

Higher prices for peak usage can be responsive to equity considerations, assuming lower-income customers have less usage that contributes to the peak. However, a peak-demand pricing system can have adverse socioeconomic effects if all of the usage during the peak period is priced at a premium rate.

The fixed portion of the water bill generally is designed to cover certain fixed costs (namely, customer-service costs) that do not vary with the level of water usage. Variable charges are used to recover variable costs as well as a considerable amount of the fixed costs of utility operations. Utility managers generally prefer to recover a high proportion of revenue require-ments from the fixed-charge component. Conservation goals tend to argue for shifting costs to the variable component of the bill.

Shifting costs from the fixed charge to the variable charge for conservation purposes can address affordability concerns. The variable component of the bill will have a greater impact on the customers with water usage that is less responsive to price. Tables 8.4 and 8.5 illustrate these effects.

A comparison of bill impacts illustrates that an across-the-board rate increase actually results in a proportionately higher increase on the urban customer. The higher the across-the-board increase, the greater the differential.

Table 8.6 provides an illustration of how two hypothetical customers in different housing situations are affected by rate changes. Although overgeneralization should be avoided, and many exceptions can be cited, residents of single-family homes often have higher incomes than apartment dwellers.

A more direct illustration of income effects is provided in Table 8.7. As discussed previously, households with lower incomes pay a higher percentage of their income for water service. For high-income households, even substantial rate increases might be considered relatively affordable from a percentage-of-income standpoint. At higher rates, the difference between income groups will be greater.

Table 8.4
Impact of price change on water bills: 40 percent increase in variable and fixed charges

	Multifamily or urban household	Single-family or suburban household
Monthly water use before rate increase	5,000 gallons	6,500 gallons
Current water bill:		
Variable charge (@ $2.50/1,000 gallons)	$12.50	$16.25
Fixed charge	$6.00	$6.00
Total water bill	$18.50	$22.25
Simplified composite price elasticity of demand (summer and winter)	−0.05	−0.10
Monthly water after rate increase	4,900 gallons	6,240 gallons
Revised bill following a 40 percent rate increase in the variable and fixed charges:		
Variable charge (@ $3.50/1,000 gallons)	$17.15	$21.84
Fixed charge	$8.40	$8.40
Total water bill	$25.55	$30.24
Percentage increase in variable charge	37.20 percent	34.40 percent
Percentage increase in total water bill	38.11 percent	35.91 percent

NOTE: Metering unit constraints are ignored.

Table 8.5
Impact of price change on water bills: 40 percent increase in variable charge and reduction in fixed charge

	Multifamily or urban household	Single-family or suburban household
Monthly water use before rate increase	5,000 gallons	6,500 gallons
Current water bill:		
Variable charge (@ $2.50/1,000 gallons)	$12.50	$16.25
Fixed charge	$8.00	$8.00
Total water bill	$18.50	$22.25
Simplified composite price elasticity of demand (summer and winter)	−0.05	−0.10
Monthly water after rate increase	4,900 gallons	6,240 gallons
Revised bill following a 40 percent rate increase in the variable and reduced fixed charges:		
Variable charge (@ $3.50/1,000 gallons)	$17.15	$21.84
Fixed charge	$4.00	$4.00
Total water bill	$21.15	$25.84
Percentage increase in variable charge	37.20 percent	34.40 percent
Percentage increase in total water bill	14.32 percent	16.13 percent

NOTE: Elasticity effects in this illustration are based on the increase in the variable charge.

Table 8.6

Impact of price change on water bills: 10, 20, and 40 percent variable charge increases

	Multiple-family or urban household	Single-family or suburban household
Monthly water use before rate increase	5,000 gallons	6,500 gallons
Current water bill:		
Variable charge (@ $2.50/1,000 gallons)	$12.50	$16.25
Simplified composite price elasticity of demand (summer and winter)	–0.05	–0.10
10-percent rate increase		
Monthly water after rate increase	4,975 gallons	6,435 gallons
Revised bill following a 10 percent rate increase in the variable charge:		
Variable charge (@ $2.75/1,000 gallons)	$13.68	$17.70
Percentage increase in total water bill	9.45 percent	8.90 percent
20-percent rate increase		
Monthly water after rate increase	4,950 gallons	6,370 gallons
Revised bill following a 20 percent rate increase in the variable charge:		
Variable charge (@ $3.00/1,000 gallons)	$14.85	$19.11
Percentage increase in total water bill	18.80 percent	17.60 percent
40-percent rate increase		
Monthly water after rate increase	4,900 gallons	6,240 gallons
Revised bill following a 40 percent rate increase in the variable charge:		
Variable charge (@ $3.50/1,000 gallons)	$17.15	$21.84
Percentage increase in total water bill	37.20 percent	34.40 percent

NOTE: These illustrations do not include fixed charges.

Block Rates

Several water utilities have introduced increasing-block rate structures to encourage conservation. An increasing-block rate requires the determination of usage blocks and rate tiers. As blocks of water usage increase, so does the unit charge for water. Higher-use households will pay an even higher water bill than under a uniform rate.

Increasing-block rates also have distributional consequences, as illustrated in Table 8.8. The rate structure can be used to shift some or all of a rate increase toward high-water-use

Table 8.7

Income effect of a price change on water bills: 10, 20, and 40 percent variable charge increases

	Lower-income household	Higher-income household
Median monthly household income	$1,500	$4,000
Current water bill:		
Variable charge (@ $2.50/1,000 gallons)	$12.50	$16.25
Percentage of income	.83 percent	.41 percent
10-percent rate increase		
Revised bill following a 10 percent rate increase in the variable charge:		
Variable charge (@ $2.75/1,000 gallons)	$13.68	$17.70
Percentage increase in total water bill	9.45 percent	8.90 percent
Percentage of income	.91 percent	.44 percent
20-percent rate increase		
Revised bill following a 20 percent rate increase in the variable charge:		
Variable charge (@ $3.00/1,000 gallons)	$14.85	$19.11
Percentage increase in total water bill	18.80 percent	17.60 percent
Percentage of income	.99 percent	.48 percent
40-percent rate increase		
Revised bill following a 40 percent rate increase in the variable charge:		
Variable charge (@ $3.50/1,000 gallons)	$17.15	$21.84
Percentage increase in total water bill	37.20 percent	34.40 percent
Percentage of income	1.14 percent	.55 percent

NOTE: These illustrations do not include fixed charges.

customers. The rationale for doing so is that high-use customers, particularly those who drive peak demand, tend to drive utility costs.

Assuming income correlates positively with water usage, increasing-block rates can be used to craft water rates that are income neutral or progressive. Under a progressive rate structure, households with higher income levels pay a higher proportion of their income to utility bills. As typically constituted, increasing-block rates help neutralize the effect of price increases. But they are not particularly progressive until the differentiation in the unit charge per block is very substantial.

Other billing options have similar effects. For example, surcharges and penalties based on a usage breakpoint can be evaluated similarly in terms of relative impact on customers. Residential

Table 8.8

Income effect of increasing-block rates

	Low water-use customer	High water-use customer
Monthly water use	4,000 gallons	8,000 gallons
Median monthly household income	$1,500	$4,000
Current water bill:		
Variable charge (@ $2.50/1,000 gallons)	$10.00	$20.00
Percentage of income	.67	.50 percent
Increasing-block rate (4,000 gallon tier)		
Variable charge block 1 (@2.50/1,000) gallons for the first 5,000 gallons	$10.00	$10.00
Variable charge block 2 (@3.00/1,000) gallons for amounts above 4,000 gallons	—	$12.00
Total water bill	$10.00	$22.00
Percentage change in total water bill	0 percent	+10.0 percent
Percentage of income	.67 percent	.55 percent
Increasing-block rate (5,000 gallon tier)		
Variable charge block 1 (@2.50/1,000) gallons for the first 5,000 gallons	$10.00	$12.50
Variable charge block 2 (@3.00/1,000) gallons for amounts above 5,000 gallons	—	$9.00
Total water bill	$10.00	$21.50
Percentage change in total water bill	0 percent	+7.5 percent
Percentage of income	.67 percent	.54 percent
Increasing-block rate (3,000 gallon tier)		
Variable charge block 1 (@2.50/1,000) gallons for the first 3,000 gallons	$7.50	$7.50
Variable charge block 2 (@3.00/1,000) gallons for amounts above 3,000 gallons	$3.00	$15.00
Total water bill	$10.50	$22.50
Percentage change in total water bill	+5.0 percent	+12.50 percent
Percentage of income	.60 percent	.56 percent
Increasing-block rate (4,000 gallon tier)		
Variable charge block 1 (@2.00/1,000) gallons for the first 4,000 gallons	$8.00	$8.00
Variable charge block 2 (@3.750/1,000) gallons for amounts above 4,000 gallons	—	$15.00
Total water bill	$8.00	$23.00
Percentage change in total water bill	-20 percent	+15 percent
Percentage of income	.53 percent	.58 percent

NOTE: These illustrations do not include fixed charges or elasticity effects.

customers with relatively inelastic demand will see their income adversely affected by the imposition of penalty charges.

Water-Budget Rates

A relatively new entrant to the available methods of conservation-oriented rate design is a rate tied to the customer's water-use requirements (also known as budget billing, water-budget billing, or goal-based rates). Like block rates, the rate varies with the amount of water used. But unlike conventional block rates, the blocks of usage vary according to some measure of customer needs—landscape evapotranspiration requirements, per-capita allotments, or variants.

The theory behind the rate is that some minimum amount of water use is required and appropriate. If this "water budget" can be defined, measured, and applied to a rate structure, a stronger price signal can be concentrated on the presumably more discretionary water use above the water budget. Customers will then have a focused incentive to use water in amounts appropriate to needs.

As illustrated in Table 8.9, households using the same amount of water will incur a different water bill if their budgeted amount is different. In the illustration, the water budget is based only on lot size, and thus the small-lot household faces a steeper rate increase. What if the small-lot, low-income household has higher residential density? The water budget then might be designed to include the number of residents, as well as lot size. The large-lot, high-income household, with the larger water budget, may have greater opportunity to conserve water, which would limit the change in their total water bill.

Water-budget rates illustrate the tradeoffs among different conceptions of equity in rate making. This type of rate can be designed to address socioeconomic concerns, but thoughtful adaptations may be needed to avoid and correct for unintended consequences.

CONCLUSIONS

Rate design is no different from other water conservation programs in that it will have socioeconomic impacts and these impacts can be assessed. For pricing, the central issue is how prices affect household income. Rate structures can be regressive, neutral, or progressive with regard to how much household income must be devoted to paying the water bill.

Table 8.9

Income effect of water-budget rates

	Household with small lot	Household with medium lot	Household with large lot
Monthly water use (no change)	6,000 gallons	6,000 gallons	10,000 gallons
Monthly budgeted water use	4,000 gallons	6,000 gallons	8,000 gallons
Median monthly household income	$1,500	$4,000	$6,000
Current water bill:			
Variable charge (@ $2.00/1,000 gallons)	$12.00	$12.00	$20.00
Percentage of income	.67%	.50 percent	.33 percent
Budget-based rate			
Variable charge block 1 (@2.00/1,000)			
based on budgeted amount	$8.00	$12.00	$16.00
Variable charge block 2 (@3.00/1,000)			
based on budgeted amount	$6.00	—	$6.00
Total water bill	$14.00	$12.00	$22.00
Percentage change in total water bill	+16.7 percent	+0.0 percent	+10.0 percent
Percentage of income	.93 percent	.50 percent	.37 percent

NOTE: These illustrations do not include fixed charges or elasticity effects.

Customers in all income brackets should receive a price signal. But for low-income households, the signal should not be disproportionately loud given their relatively low water use, less capacity to conserve, and constrained ability to pay. At the other end of the spectrum are customers who use more water (especially peak-period water), have a greater capacity to conserve, and have ability to bear a greater share of water-system costs.

Taking socioeconomic factors into account, it becomes clear that although pricing is an essential component of a conservation strategy, it might not yield the expected water savings. For low-income customers, responses to price changes are constrained because the bulk of water use is for basic needs and because low-income households have limited capital to invest in more-efficient water-use fixtures. For high-income customers, these same constraints do not exist, but there is a propensity for greater utilization of water-consuming appliances and landscapes—and a greater ability to pay higher prices. By analyzing socioeconomic impacts, utilities can craft rate-design policies that help achieve efficiency and equity goals. Combining pricing with programmatic conservation efforts may allow utilities to choose among a variety of options for mitigating the adverse effects of rate increase on low-income customers.

CHAPTER 9

PROGRAM DESIGN AND IMPLEMENTATION

INTRODUCTION

As discussed throughout this report, designing effective conservation programs requires attention to the potential impact of socioeconomic conditions on water usage, conservation, and conservation programs. Moreover, utilities can follow some strategies to design programs that recognize and respond to socioeconomic conditions in the service territory.

This chapter concerns design and implementation issues for programs that simultaneously address water conservation and socioeconomic considerations.

PROGRAM TARGETING

The concept of targeted conservation captures the idea that water conservation programs can—and possibly should—target the conditions and needs of the low-income population. Two strong rationales for targeted conservation can be made. First, water savings that can be translated into savings on the customer's bill address affordability concerns. Second, the housing conditions of low-income populations often suffer from outdated or substandard plumbing fixtures. Repairs and replacements, therefore, tend to produce the "biggest bang for the buck." Earlier chapters introduced the concept of targeting, and this section provides an overview of implementation strategies for targeted programs.

The potential savings can be established by conducting water audits of low-income housing properties. Whole-house audits can be used to jointly assess the potential savings from energy- and water-efficiency improvements. The incremental cost of a water audit in addition to an energy audit is usually not large. Audits yield valuable information to utilities and customers, while also providing opportunities for simple repairs and education about water conservation practices.

Implementing a residential water conservation audit is not necessarily as costly as an energy audit. Water conservation generally does not require special capital requirements or financing arrangements, as in the case of weatherization and retrofit programs in the energy sector. Water-use audits, educational materials, and certain plumbing repairs can be provided at the time of the audit. Many water-saving devices are inexpensive and easy to install. Consumer education can be used to encourage changes in water-use habits, which can result in substantial water savings.

Even water utilities with plentiful supplies and low costs may want to consider implementing conservation programs targeted at the low-income population. Grants or other forms of community assistance may be available for targeted conservation efforts. Such programs can be cost effective if they present a viable alternative to disconnecting customers that adds to revenue losses and instability. Special programs also have the potential for added benefits in terms of enhancing customer bill-payment and building positive community relations.

Targeted conservation serves another purpose in the context of affordability programs. Many utilities are reluctant to simply provide discounts or special rates to low-income or fixed-income customers because of the concern that incentives for efficient use will be lost. However, conservation activities can be a quid pro quo for a rate or other discount. These arrangements are not unlike modern welfare programs and reflect the belief that beneficiaries should play an active role in programs addressing their needs as a condition for receiving subsidies.

The consideration of socioeconomic impacts in the context of water conservation efforts always highlights an important lesson: For individual households, there is a big difference between saving water and saving dollars.

Given rising costs, historic underpricing of water service, and the pressing need to send customers an appropriate price signal about water, the total water bill for many customers may rise even with diligent conservation actions and behavior. A program with a socioeconomic dimension and targeting can address this concern.

Most conservation programs are geared toward saving water within households, but they also reduce total demand (or "load") on the water system as a whole. Strategic water conservation can help water systems avoid costs by targeting areas where system costs are greatest. Generally, the benefits and costs of conservation are focused at the aggregate system level. For system-wide efficiency, the utility will want to target high, wasteful, and extraordinary water usage—regardless of where it might be found across the socioeconomic strata of the service population.

Practitioners who recognize the benefits of targeting have affirmed this last point. However, targeting does not diminish the benefits of a broad-based approach to water conservation:

> Targeting those who have the most potential for savings is worth the extra effort on the first few rounds of a program. However, there are other values to establish and benefits to receive in contacting and evaluating all customers. Such as those who are doing a good job of managing their water consumption need to know how and where they are doing a good job. Positive reinforcement of the core water use values is essential to maintaining a good water use ethic.[*]

Programs with a customer-income component focus attention on the affordability of water to individual households. Under some circumstances, water conservation programs targeted at a specific group of customers may not produce a substantial impact in terms of water savings. Given that water usage is income elastic, low-income customers do not necessarily contribute substantially to total system demand. Nonetheless, the impact on those customers in terms of improved ability to pay for water service, and avoided late payments and disconnections, may be quite significant.

Based on the findings throughout this study, Table 9.1 provides several program design considerations based on generalized differences between low-income and high-income households along several criteria.

It is appropriate to include an estimate of these benefits to households and to the utility in an evaluation. Reductions in nonpayment and disconnection can be estimated for the utility. These savings benefit all utility customers by reducing the cost of operations. However, it also is worth recognizing the benefits to the individual household of maintaining water service.

Utilities should bear in mind the difference between saving water and saving dollars when designing conservation and assistance programs. Programs that seek primarily to save water should target higher-income groups, where water usage is proportionately higher (for example, customers with large, water-consumptive landscapes). However, utilities that want to improve affordability should target some programs to lower-income groups. For these programs, effectiveness cannot be measured in aggregate water savings alone but also must be assessed in terms of how well the program accomplishes household water efficiency and affordability goals.

---

[*] Interview with Paul Freestone, AWWA Conservation Committee.

Table 9.1

Program-design considerations based on generalized differences

between low-income and high-income households

	Low-income households	High-income households
Water usage	Indoor end uses, which are less price responsive, may account for a high proportion of water consumption; leakage rates can be significant for older housing.	Outdoor end uses, which are more price responsive, may account for a high proportion of water consumption; indoor uses also can be significant due to water-using fixtures and appliances. Tend to have higher levels of water use.
Responsiveness to price signals	Water usage may be somewhat less price responsive but more income responsive; households may not be directly billed for water services.	Higher-income households may be somewhat less price responsive than households having similar levels of use but lower income.
Price impacts	Price increases aggravate affordability problems; conservation programs, as well as bill-payment assistance, monthly billing, and other methods can improve affordability in the wake of increases.	Usage may be less responsive to price changes at higher income levels; may be important to augment price changes with consumer information and education.
Participation issues	Lack of program awareness can be a barrier; up-front program costs can prevent participation; targeting programs can improve access and participation rates.	Participation rates may be higher in general; potential for free riders can be addressed in program design.
Effect of conservation on households	Can significantly reduce household water bills and improve affordability.	Can help reduce household water usage; bill reduction can be significant under increasing-block rates.
Effect of conservation on utility	Can help reduce average water usage and lower associated costs; can improve community relations and improve bill-payment behavior.	Can help reduce both average and peak-period water usage and lower associated costs; peak-demand reductions may be particularly beneficial to the utility.

The ideal program design identifies and integrates conservation and socioeconomic impact goals prior to implementation.

PROGRAM STRATEGIES

This section presumes that the water utility manager wants to (1) implement a conservation program that recognizes socioeconomic characteristics; (2) use conservation strategies to address a socioeconomic condition, namely the ability of customers to afford water service; and/ or (3) mitigate adverse socioeconomic impacts that might occur with some conservation-oriented programs.

Water utilities can take a gradual approach to implementing a conservation program with a socioeconomic dimension. This will allow the utility to assess the program's effectiveness, fine-tune program elements, and expand or contract efforts based on experiences and results.

Utility managers can follow some basic steps in approaching this issue: assess existing data and information, collect additional information, promote awareness throughout the utility organization, modify existing programs and activities, develop a pilot program, and implement a full program.

Assess the Data

Most utilities have already collected more information about their customers than they realize. As a first step, internal data sources should be evaluated. These data include

- Bill-payment behavior and trends
- Arrearages, late payments, and uncollectable accounts
- Customer attitude surveys
- Evaluation data from existing efforts (effectiveness)
- Qualitative evaluations by customer service staff about needs and issues

This last point cannot be overemphasized. The utility workers on the "front line"— customer-service personnel at payment centers and conservation program staff who work directly with customers—often are in the best position to evaluate conditions and needs.

Utilities also will want to gather information about the service territory. Utilities can use federal, state, and local resources to compile basic socioeconomic characteristics, including but not limited to

- Average and median family income
- Families and persons below the poverty level (and other thresholds)

- Household size characteristics
- Property values (and average size)
- Ethnicity and cultural characteristics

The U.S. Census Bureau (www.census.gov) and state departments of commerce and community development often provide excellent starting points. Today, these data also can be examined spatially using geographic information systems. This can facilitate an understanding of variations in the service territory across units as small as neighborhoods.

Utilities should keep in mind that socioeconomic conditions are dynamic. Collecting and assessing socioeconomic data should be ongoing. Furthermore, flexible programs can respond to inevitable changes in utility service territories.

Promote Awareness

Laying the groundwork for a program requires building awareness throughout the utility organization. This may require additional staffing, as well as additional training for staff. It also may require better integration of utility personnel working in different departments and locations.

Methods to build awareness include forming a task force or work group, providing training opportunities and resource materials, and exchanging information among departments. Staff members need opportunities to share "war stories" and success stories. A task force or work group that meets informally but regularly can begin to identify needs and formulate strategies.

Customer-service personnel may need training in how basic water conservation measures work and how to convey this information to customers. Similarly, water conservation program personnel may need training in how to recognize and respond to different types of customers with different needs.

Utility staff should be encouraged to interact and share ideas that could make conservation and assistance programs more effective. In fact, a "bottom-up" versus a "top-down" approach to defining the problem and crafting solutions might prove more effective in the long run. Early and active participation by employees in program development efforts will help inform the process as

146

well as acknowledge the vital role of the staff in implementation. Moreover, staff members who feel they have a stake in the program's success will work hard toward that end.

For some utilities, a need may exist to build awareness among "street-level" personnel who interface with customers on a day-to-day basis. For others, a need may exist to build awareness in the upper management. Building awareness throughout the organization is essential.

In addition to promoting awareness within the utility organization, it may also be important to build awareness within the community at large, including the media, government agencies, and elected officials.

Modify Existing Programs and Activities

Building on the data assessment and increased awareness in the organization, the utility can begin to modify existing programs and activities. Some existing programs may already demonstrate a record of success; others may reveal deficiencies. Attention should be paid to programs that are not producing expected results or for which the utility is concerned about unintended adverse consequences.

For existing customer-assistance programs, personnel can offer information and low-cost water-saving kits to customers that visit utility payment centers. Customers having difficulty paying their water bill can be counseled about conservation strategies. Payment plans can be used to keep customers on the system as they work to help lower their water bills through conservation.

Similarly, conservation programs can be "retooled" to address socioeconomic considerations. Materials printed in English, for example, can also be produced in Spanish or other languages spoken in the community. Conservation programs can be tailored to the needs of socioeconomic groups. Rebate and other programs can be assessed in terms of socioeconomic impacts, and possibly modified to address affordability and distributional considerations.

A key strategy for many utilities is to work to integrate programs and activities. The conservation manager and the customer-assistance manager may find it mutually beneficial to share data and develop joint strategies. True integration may require changes in organization, staffing, and information systems.

In addition, utilities can use existing programs and activities to interact with customers through interviews and feedback surveys to ascertain the level of customer interest in programs. Focus groups and other techniques also can be used to assess customer needs and preferences.

Develop a Pilot Program

When considering the introduction of new utility programs, a pilot program can be beneficial. Pilots can be especially helpful when designing programs that address socioeconomic considerations. During the course of the pilot, utilities can learn what works and what does not work, as well as whether programs have unexpected impacts on customers.

A pilot program generally is defined in terms of implementing the program on a limited basis, for a limited time, or in a limited geographic area. A pilot is essentially a policy experiment. The key to a successful pilot program is in the design of appropriate evaluation instruments. The pilot results should be evaluated in terms of all relevant benefits and costs associated with the program. Utilities should evaluate quantitative data but also make use of qualitative feedback from customers, utility staff members, and others who may be affected by the program or involved in its implementation.

A pilot program might require the approval of city officials or regulatory agencies. An unsuccessful program may require the utility to go "back to the drawing board." Results of the pilot should be used in design and implementation of a full program.

Implement a Full Program

A pilot program, or series of programs, can be expanded into a full ongoing program. Nonetheless, even a "permanent" program can be approached experimentally. The goals of the program in terms of both water conservation and socioeconomic impacts must be well articulated.

As discussed in the previous chapters, efficiency and cost-effectiveness can guide the program-design process. The program should target activities that will yield the best results, based on program goals, at the lowest possible cost. Benefits and costs should be assessed in the course of implementation to see if expected results (and unexpected results) occur.

A full program requires attention to eligibility and participation issues. It also requires resources for implementation. The utility will need to identify a funding source, assign staff, and gain approvals from oversight bodies. It may be necessary and desirable to partner with a community-based organization to facilitate program implementation. These and other broader implementation issues are discussed in the next section.

The program should build in data-collection and evaluation components to provide feedback to utility managers that will be essential to assessing goal achievement and impacts, and fine-tuning the program. As discussed previously, evaluation methods can be expanded to include both conservation and socioeconomic impacts (both intended and unintended).

Figure 9.1 summarizes the basic steps to implementing a full program. Each step requires an additional level of effort and raises policy issues (Table 9.2). Ongoing evaluation can help systems assess impacts and modify programs over time.

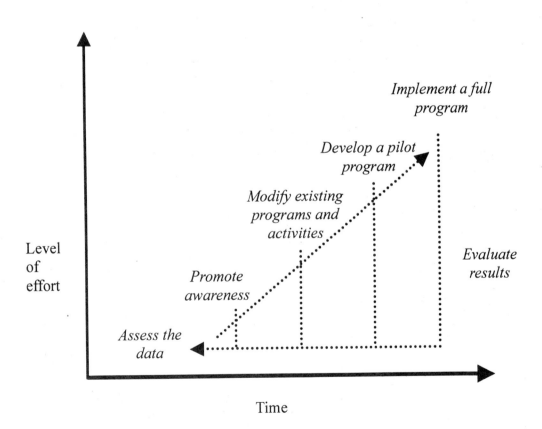

Figure 9.1   Steps to building a program

Table 9.2

Implementation steps and issues

Basic steps	Associated issues
Assess internal data	Availability of data
	Quality of data
	Coordination within utility
	Consumer privacy issues
	Spatial presentation of data
Build awareness	Awareness throughout organization
	Coordination among departments
	Training needs
	Community outreach and feedback
Modify existing programs and activities	Assess current programs in terms of intended and unintended outcomes
	Compare existing efforts to those of nearby or similar utilities (benchmarking)
	Introduce conservation component to assistance efforts
	Introduce socioeconomic considerations to conservation programs
	Define a broad range of programmatic alternatives
Conduct a pilot program	Define the target
	Customer involvement
	Data collection
	Evaluation criteria and tools
	Qualitative and quantitative assessment
Implement a full program	Eligibility requirements
	Funding
	Partnering
	Staffing and organization
	Regulatory issues

IMPLEMENTATION ISSUES

Utility conservation programs involve a host of implementation issues. Incorporating socioeconomic considerations will add some issues, but nothing that a well-planned program cannot readily handle.

Eligibility

When utilities decide to target a program to low-income households, eligibility criteria are needed. Utilities must determine eligibility criteria for programs. Various government-assistance programs use federal income guidelines when determining eligibility for assistance. The federal poverty guidelines (or a percentage thereof) can be used to identify qualifying households (see Table 9.3).

Another issue for utilities that implement programs directed to the needs of low-income households is respecting personal privacy. Customers may be reluctant to divulge income, employment, citizenship status, and related information to the utilities. For this reason, utilities may want to defer to community-assistance agencies, or other local utilities with income-based programs, to determine program eligibility. Alternatively, eligibility can be based on whether the household qualifies for some other form of assistance such as Transitional Aid to Needy Families, which replaced Aid to Families with Dependent Children, or the Low-Income Home Energy Assistance Program.

Eligibility for renters or others who do not pay the water bill directly can be considered. Ideally, the utility program will reach landlords and tenants when targeting multifamily properties for conservation activities.

Utilities must exercise caution when using income, water usage, and other personal data for program evaluation purposes. Respecting and safeguarding the customer's privacy should be a priority because it is essential for building a relationship of trust with customers.

Table 9.3

Federal poverty guidelines (Year 2000)

Household size			
1	$ 8,350	$10,430	$ 9,590
2	11,250	14,060	12,930
3	14,150	17,690	16,270
4	17,050	21,320	19,610
5	19,950	24,950	22,950
6	22,850	8,580	226,290
7	25,750	32,210	29,630
8	28,650	35,840	32,970
For each additional person, add	2,900	3,630	3,340

Source: U.S. Department of Health and Human Services, The 2000 HHS Poverty Guidelines
http://aspe.hhs.gov/poverty/00poverty.htm.

Participation

All water conservation programs depend on customer participation for success. Ideally, the program will induce interest in conservation on the part of customers who would otherwise not participate. Similarly, the utility generally wants to limit the number of free riders who partake in program benefits, even though they would have implemented conservation measures on their own and without special utility incentives.

Utilities will want to pay special attention to how their programs invite participation from groups for which the program would be particularly beneficial. Some simple strategies can be used to enhance participation. Program success is more likely if community members are involved in program design. Another important strategy is to communicate through appropriate materials, paying attention to language, accessibility, and availability. Finally, utilities can employ local residents for program implementation.

For low-income and fixed-income households or other households with special circumstances, it is important for the utility to lower the cost of participation. Although a rebate program might work for the general service population, low-income customers might be excluded from participation if the up-front cost is prohibitive. A "free" program may prove to be more far more effective in raising the level of participation. Utilities might consider special financing or repayment options; in some cases, a no-cost option could yield positive results.

The time required for participation is another type of cost. For example, working-class families may not have the time or resources to pick up a conservation kit during the utility's regular business hours. Utilities can make kits available in the neighborhoods where people live and work.

The benefits of enhancing opportunities for participation extend beyond program effectiveness. With each positive encounter, the utility is building valuable relationships with customers.

Funding

Funding for conservation and assistance efforts can come from internal or external sources. Internal sources are generated within the utility, while external sources come from public or private sources outside of the utility. According to a leading program manager:

152

There is tremendous power in partnership, often with organizations with which you would otherwise not have anything in common. I am currently working on a $12 million grant proposal to create a new education and job placement program for youth in the city's "empowerment" zone. (Inner city and low socioeconomic areas with high juvenile crime and school drop out.)

What does it have to do with water conservation? It's my ticket to creating a small business incubator for young entrepreneurs to install and maintain Xeriscape™ landscaping. The training ground will be the same homes we made water efficient with Neighbors Helping Neighbors. We can't do this on our own, but by partnering with a dozen city and non-city groups, we may get my landscape program and a strong program to train future water wise landscapers. Indirectly, the U.S. Department of Education is going to help us do low-water landscaping on several hundred low-income homes—and train kids from the same neighborhood to replicate the same type of landscapes elsewhere. Getting potential gang members off the street and making them taxpayers is a bonus—but it counts as a benefit just like not doing so counts as a cost to the city.[*]

Partnering is never easy. It takes time and energy to build and maintain the partnership; there are many egos to feed and many perspectives to consider. But it's worth it if it makes a program happen that would not otherwise.

Internal funding for utilities generally comes from utility rate revenues. Lifeline rate structures and special conservation or assistance programs funded with utility revenues tend to raise the issue of subsidization from "other" ratepayers. However, utilities provide various subsidies to certain customer types (such as economic development rates to industrial customers) because the subsidized activity is perceived as beneficial to the community. In the case of low-income programs, the benefits in terms of affordability, public health, and goodwill are appreciable. Moreover, the cost of program funding should be compared with the costs associated with bad debt, collections, and disconnection.

Special rate structures can achieve multiple policy goals while also providing a source of subsidies and program funding. A conservation-oriented lifeline rate, for example, keeps a block of basic water usage more affordable to customers while recovering more costs from higher rates

---

[*] Interview with Thomas Babcock, Phoenix Water Services Department.

at higher usage levels.* In the context of this analysis, a lifeline rate helps mitigate the effects of higher rates necessary to reflect true costs and induce wise use. Conservation-oriented surcharges or penalties can be earmarked to fund special programs. Obviously, any change to the rate structure must be evaluated in terms of established rate-making criteria, including revenue sufficiency and stability for the utility. But the range of acceptable options appears to be expanding.

Following the experience of electric utilities, some water utilities raise funds through voluntary contributions from customers. Customers typically can check a box on their water bill to contribute a dollar or more for the program. In many cases, the administration of funds is handled by an outside agency that also helps implement the program.

Grants from government or even private sources might be available for program funding in some areas. Grants may cover some, but not all, utility expenses or provide seed money for a new program that eventually must become self-sufficient.

Staffing

A first step in organizing and staffing a program is to assess and coordinate in-house capability. In some cases, staffing is more a matter of *mobilizing* existing staff than of adding new staff or capability. Partnering with local energy utilities, assistance agencies, and other community-based organizations can help lower program costs and increase effectiveness.

Customers that qualify for energy service assistance might be considered eligible for water service assistance. Households having difficulty paying for one bill often will find it difficult to pay others. Water utilities and energy utilities could coordinate education, home audit, and retrofit efforts. Saving water and energy go hand in hand, particularly in terms of hot water usage in the home.

Any utility program can bring jobs into a community. Even temporary jobs provide a source of training in addition to temporary income. Training for staff should be broad-based and include not only technical training, but training in communication skills, record keeping, personal safety, and any other skills necessary for the program. Low-income housing can pose challenges

---

* As water prices rise to reflect true costs, lifeline rate making may become a more important tool. Although they may trade off a degree of efficiency in the price signal, this effect can be countered with an effective education program.

for field staff. Staff members should be prepared for working in various conditions and circumstances and empowered to make decisions in the field that ensure their well-being as well as that of the program.

Utilities may find that community-based organizations can provide not only access to targeted customer groups but potential program staffing as well. The San Diego County Water Authority, for example, used community-based organizations to distribute ULFTs tto customers. The program was able to reach customers who traditionally did not participate in water conservation programs and also provided employment opportunities for community residents. In this respect, the training and employment aspects of a conservation program, a targeted program, can be consistent with local goals of citizen empowerment.

Another potential organization and staffing strategy is to contract out with a vendor who is willing to implement the program. Some vendors might be willing to engage in a performance contract, where payment is tied to benchmarks for success (participation rates, water savings, etc.). Private vendors also can be required to employ local residents in the field.

Approval

Significant modifications to existing programs, pilot programs, and full programs will require the approval of an oversight body.

For municipal water utilities, a water board or city council might be briefed about the need for a program, opportunities and goals, funding and staffing, and other aspects of the program. An assessment of potential benefits and costs and a plan for actual results are essential. It also may be important for decision makers to understand that the program will be approached experimentally, so necessary adjustments can be made.

For water utilities regulated by state public utility commissions, particularly investor-owned water systems, significant expenditures and changes to billing practices or rate structures require approval of the state public utility commission. Commissions tend to assess such proposals on a case-by-case basis and in the larger context of impacts on all ratepayers.

The utility that can provide sufficient evidence of benefits relative to costs has a higher chance of approval. Reductions in uncollectible accounts, arrearages, and disconnection expenses will be relevant. The commissions are not likely to stand in the way of programs funded by shareholders or through voluntary contributions, or programs involving coordination of limited efforts with social assistance agencies.

STARTING FROM SCRATCH:
STRATEGIES FOR UTILITIES WITHOUT PROGRAMS

Implementation strategies depend in part on the utility's current activities. Utilities in regions considered "water-rich," such as the Midwest, may be somewhat cautious about investing heavily in conservation. As discussed previously, however, the benefits of some basic conservation-oriented activities may be well worth the cost.

Utilities that are not presently implementing a conservation program can begin by exploring some basic strategies targeted to the needs of customers who are having difficulty paying their bills. Program strategies that might be explored include

- Conduct an assessment of socioeconomic conditions in the service territory.
- Evaluate socioeconomic impacts of existing programs and activities, including existing rate structures.
- Consider billing alternatives, including monthly and budget billing.
- Consult with community-based organizations experienced with working with various groups within the service territory.
- Collaborate with local energy utilities for joint energy-water assistance programs, including conservation component.
- Work with local plumbing firms and retailers to provide low-cost repairs and retrofits.
- Train customer service personnel in basic water conservation techniques so they can provide information to customers.
- Encourage conservation personnel to incorporate socioeconomic considerations in their programs.
- Make basic conservation kits available to low-income customers or distribute them through local service or charitable organizations.

- Establish a voluntary $1 contribution for a low-income assistance program that could be administered by a local service agency.
- Explore available grant support for developing or implementing a program.
- Design a limited pilot conservation program targeted to the low-income population.

CONCLUSIONS

Water utilities can take an incremental and experimental approach to address the joint goals of water conservation and responsiveness to the needs of low-income households and other customer groups. Successful programs can be built gradually on modest achievements in modified programs and pilots.

Utilities should be prepared to return to the drawing board, perhaps more than once, in the course of implementation. Utilities with the best intentions and a good program on paper may experience unexpected problems in the actual process of implementation. Evaluation tools, including feedback from customers and staff members, will be invaluable in modifying the program.

Program goals should balance ambition and optimism with pragmatism. Remember that although water savings in an individual household may be relatively small relative to the entire capacity of the system, even small reductions can mean the difference between a bill that is affordable and one that is not. Indeed, many small reductions can add up to a sizable program effect.

APPENDIX A

CASE STUDY SUMMARIES AND PROTOCOL

CITY OF LOS ANGELES, CALIFORNIA, DEPARTMENT OF WATER AND POWER

Overview

The Department of Water and Power (DWP) serves the City of Los Angeles and some small adjacent areas. The service area receives approximately 12 inches of precipitation annually. The DWP obtains 30 percent of its supply from surface sources and 20 percent from ground sources, with the residual being purchased from the Metropolitan Water District of Southern California. The DWP has a service area of 469 square miles and serves a population of 3,700,000 (in 1997 with approximately 665,000 customers). It has approximately 463,000 residential customers, 118,000 multifamily residential customers, 60,000 commercial customers, 7,400 industrial customers, and 7,000 governmental customers. The DWP supplied 614.5 thousand acre-feet of water in 1995–1996 with an annual per capita consumption of 50,200 gallons, or 137 gallons per capita per day. About 60 percent of total water consumption is accounted for by residential customers, 25 percent by commercial and governmental sectors, and 4 percent by industry. (The remaining amount was used for fire-fighting or lost through evaporation, system leaks, and breaks.)[*] This information is summarized in Table A.1.

Conservation Programs

The City of Los Angeles DWP has a long history designing and developing some of the largest-scale conservation programs in the country (Table A.2).

---

[*] Urban Water Management Plan, *Annual Update Report, LADWP,* February 1997.

Summary characteristics for Los Angeles Department of Water and Power

Region	City of Los Angeles and some adjacent areas
Annual rainfall	12 inches
Size of service area	469 square miles
Population of service area	3,700,000 in 1997
Number of customer accounts	665,000
Single-family residential customers	463,000
Multifamily residential customers	118,000
Commercial customers	60,000
Industrial customers	7,400
Amount of water supplied	614.5 thousand acre-feet in 1995–1996
Per-capita consumption	50,200 gallons annually; 137 gallons per day
Composition of water demand	60 percent residential customers; 25 percent commercial and governmental customers; 4 percent industrial customers
Composition of water supply	60–70 percent from surface sources; 13–18 percent from ground sources; residual purchased from the Metropolitan Water District of Southern California

Source: Based on materials provided by Los Angeles Department of Water and Power.

Conservation Assistance Program for Low-Income Customers

The Conservation Assistance Program was implemented for 6 months in 1991. It began in response to a customer-service survey and aimed at targeting low-income customers. The program was a large-scale effort that distributed conservation kits and information by mail to a targeted group of 60,000 single-family water customers. The mailing of these kits was implemented by using a "three-contact" marketing approach to get customer attention. First, a postcard alerting the customer of the impending arrival of the conservation kit was sent. The kit was mailed 1 week later; an announcement that assistance with installation would be made available upon request was mailed 2 weeks after the kit.

Ultra Low-Flush Toilet Community-Based Organization

The Ultra-Low-Flush (ULF) Program began in 1992 in an attempt to reach customers not taking advantage of the ULF Rebate Program. The program was community based, employing

Table A.2

Summary of conservation programs at Los Angeles Department of Water and Power

	Targeted programs			Untargeted residential programs			
	Cons. Assist. Program	U.L.F. Toilet C.B.O.	Community Cons. Partnership	Showerhead Distribution	U.L.F. Toilet Rebate	Home Water Survey	In Concert with the Environment
Inception date	1991	1992	1995	1988	1990	1991	1995
Duration	6 months	current	5–6 months				
Impetus	Responses to attitude survey: customer service	1. Political drivers 2. Increasing toilet distribution	Legislative inducement	Sewer constraints and water supply concerns	Drought: Toilets viewed as producing predictable savings, require no behavioral change	Drought: Residential surveys viewed as providing customer service and water savings	BMP Driven
Goals	Reach low income	Reach those not using rebate prog.	Comply with mandate and save water	Decrease sewer flow and reduce consumptive demand			
Design and implementation difficulty (1=very easy 10=very difficult)	3	5	Design = 7 Implem. = 10	Design = 4 Implem. = 9	Design = 4 Implem. = 8	Design = 4 Implem. = 6	Design = 3 Implem. = 5
Program modifications	Few	Some	Many	Few	Some	Major changes	Some
Financing	DWP rate structure includes a pass through to fund demand-side management and reclamation projects (since 1993)						
Overall program effectiveness	6	8	3–5	8	10	7–8	8–9
Customer response	7	8–9	5	8	9–10	6–7	9

Source: Based on materials provided by Los Angeles Department of Water and Power.

previously unemployed members of the target community to market and distribute the ULF toilets. This program was successful because residents were receptive to the community members in charge of the local operations.

Community Conservation Partnership Program

The Community Conservation Partnership (CCP) Program was implemented for 5 to 6 months in 1995. The program targeted single-family residents as well as apartment owners and managers in the service region with Home Water Surveys. This service included the direct installation of up to two new ULFTs, low-flow showerheads, and faucet aerators in the homes of senior citizens and low-income customers. Customers were educated regarding additional conservation opportunities, and apartment managers were encouraged to pass on the information to their residents

Utility Rate Structure and History

The DWP has an increasing-block rate structure (with two tiers) that applies to all customer classes. The first-tier rate includes a revenue-adjustment factor that assures that a targeted minimum revenue will be collected. It also includes passthrough adjustment factors for water procurement and water-quality improvements. The second-tier rate is based on marginal cost and has a seasonal component. Peak second-tier rates are applicable to usage in June through October; off-peak second-tier rates are applicable to usage in November through May. The formula for determining first-tier usage for peak and off-peak periods varies with customer class.

For single-family residential customers, the breakpoint between first- and second-tier usage is based on lot size (five categories), temperature zone (three zones), and household size (the household adjustment involves a sliding scale of allowed extra first-tier usage for households of 7 to households of 13 or more). For multifamily residential customers, all usage in the off-peak period is billed at the first-tier rate; usage in the peak period in excess of 125 percent of the previous average winter usage for December through March is billed at the second-tier rate.

A similar rate structure is applicable to commercial and industrial customers, as well as to governmental customers. However, nonsingle-family residential customers with high seasonal variation in usage as well as large turf customers that have achieved maximum practical reductions in usage via conservation practices may apply to have 95 percent of their usage in the peak period billed at the first-tier rate. The City of Los Angeles Department of Public Works sets wastewater rates; the sewage charge is based on metered water usage, with a standard exemption for water not returned to the sewers (i.e., outdoor usage).

DWP also has a lifeline rate available to low-income or senior/disabled customers. Income eligibility is determined by an adjusted gross income (AGI) threshold, currently set to a household AGI of $20,500 or less. To qualify, customers submit a Lifeline Rate Application to the city clerk with a copy of the previous year's tax return for verification.

CITY OF PHOENIX, ARIZONA, PHOENIX WATER SERVICES DEPARTMENT

Overview

The Phoenix Water Services Department (PWSD) provides service to the City of Phoenix, a portion of Paradise Valley, and several customers in Maricopa County. The service area receives approximately 7 inches of rainfall annually. Phoenix obtains 94 percent of its supply from surface sources (via purchases from the Central Arizona Project [CAP] and the Salt River Project) and obtains the residual from ground sources. The PWSD has a service area of 530 square miles and serves a population of 1,215,000 (in 1996–1997 with approximately 318,000 customer accounts). It has approximately 278,000 single-family residential customers, 16,000 multifamily residential customers, 23,800 commercial customers, and 220 industrial customers.

The PWSD supplied approximately 313,000 acre-feet of water in 1996–1997 with an annual per-capita consumption of approximately 230 gallons per capita per day. The composition of this usage was single-family residential (51 percent), multifamily residential (18 percent), commercial (27 percent), and industrial (4 percent). This information is summarized in Table A.3.

Summary characteristics for Phoenix Water Services Department

Region	City of Phoenix, portions of Paradise Valley and Maricopa County
Annual rainfall	7.5 inches (4.25 inches from 1996–1997)
Size of service area	530 square miles
Population of service area	1.215 million in 1996–1997
Number of customer accounts	318,000
Single-family residential customers	278,185
Multifamily residential customers	16,330
Commercial customers	23,800
Industrial customers	220
Amount of water supplied	313,000 acre feet in 1996–1997
Annual per-capita consumption	230 gallons per day
Composition of demand	51 percent single-family residential; 18 percent multifamily residential; 27 percent commercial; 4 percent industrial
Composition of supply	94 percent from surface sources

Source: Based on materials provided by Phoenix Water Services Department.

Targeted Conservation Programs

Phoenix's targeted water conservation programs are described below and summarized in Table A.4.

Low-Income Program, Human Services Department, Program

The Low-Income Program, implemented in 1988–1989, was a labor-intensive hands-on plumbing-repair program used for those customers who qualified for assistance with their water bills. It was intended to help offset the impact of rising water rates on low-income households. The services and assistance were provided through the City of Phoenix Human Services Department (HSD). No plumbing replacements or repiping were involved with this program.

Seniors Helping Seniors Program

The Seniors Helping Seniors (SHS) Program, which began in 1989, is mainly an audit program that uses teams of senior volunteers to install conservation measures and provide energy

Table A.4

Summary of targeted conservation programs at Phoenix Water Services Department

	Low Income Program HSD	Seniors	Union Hill	Utility Assistance Program (HSD)	Neighbors Helping Neighbors (MetroTech)
Inception Date	1988–1989	1989	1990–1992	1990	1994
Duration	1 year	current	2 years	current	current
Impetus	Piggy back on Emergency Weatherization Program	State agency and nonprofit seniors organization	CAP shutdown threat	Concern about affordability	Concern about affordability
Goals	Helping low income customers at low cost	Serve under-served customers	Emergency Demand Reduction	Maintain water service Save water	Maintain water service Save water
Design and Implementation Difficulty 1 = very easy 10 = very difficult	3–4	3–4	9	5	7–8
Program Modifications	Some	Few	Few	Few	Many
Financing	Water Res. Acq. Fee (WRAF) and Wastewater (WW) funding	WRAF, WW, state grant	WRAF, WW	WRAF, WW	WRAF, WW, state and federal funding
Overall Program Effectiveness	8	9	8	9	10
Effectiveness in Saving Water	1–2	4	9	3	4–5
Customer Response	10	8–10	8–10	8	9

Source: Based on materials provided by Phoenix Water Services Department.

education to other senior residents. The SHS Program measures address water and energy conservation, education, health, and safety issues. Water-saving equipment, such as low-flow showerheads, toilet tank water-displacement devices, and replacement flappers, are installed when necessary. Additional services include installation of water heater jackets, pipe insulation, caulking, weather stripping, and door sweeps, as well as insulating gaskets for switch and outlet plates. When necessary, volunteers adjust the water heater thermostat to a more appropriate lower setting, install smoke detectors, and repair or replace door locks.

Personal counseling to discuss the measures that were implemented is provided, and handbooks are provided for future reference. In addition to these individual assistance methods, educational programs are conducted at senior centers to provide training, educational handouts, and conservation-products information. The program uses a partnership of local government and community groups to provide support within the community, demonstrating the necessary cooperation between government entities, the private sector, and nonprofit organizations.

Union Hill Project

The Union Hill Project, implemented from 1990–1992, was a hands-on, city-installed conservation effort. It was implemented in response to a CAP shutdown threat and undertaken to drastically reduce water demand. CAP has been delivering water to the City of Phoenix since operations at the Union Hills Water Treatment Plant began in 1986. The program used low-flow showerheads and toilet tank water-displacement devices in its conservation effort.

Utility Assistance Program

The Utility Assistance Program began in 1990. It is a hands-on repair and upgrade program targeted at lower income customers. It assists residents who fall behind in paying their utility bills. Contributions from customers and water department funds are used to pay water bills for eligible low-income clients. The program was implemented in an attempt to maintain service to qualifying households as well as an effort to reduce water usage.

The Neighbors Helping Neighbors (NHN) Program was developed in 1994 to address concerns about water affordability. It was implemented in an attempt to assist inner-city residents in maintaining their service so as to achieve water conservation and provide job training and employment opportunities to local residents. Free water-saving devices, including low-flow showerheads, faucets, and toilet-tank displacement devices, are installed by students in the plumbing program at MetroTech Vocational High School.

Untargeted Conservation Programs

Phoenix's untargeted water conservation programs are described below and summarized in Table A.5.

Emergency Retrofit Program

The Emergency Retrofit Program was implemented in 1985 by the Phoenix Water and Wastewater Department (PWWD) in response to an excess sewer flow in part of northern Phoenix.* A potential crisis could occur if the sewers backed up, perhaps into individual homes in the area. The two-year program attempted to reduce sewer flows in the area by distributing free low-flow showerheads and toilet-tank dams; installation was provided upon request. A public information program was implemented in conjunction with the distribution hardware and aimed at reducing water use through a voluntary effort to reduce water demand.

Retrofit Program

The Retrofit Program was executed in 1989–1990 in an attempt to implement the 1986 conservation plan. The goal of the program was to conserve water with very little cost. The

---

* *Phoenix Emergency Retrofit Program: Impacts on Water Use and Consumer Behavior*, prepared by the Planning and Management Consultants, Ltd. and PWWD, June 1988.

Summary of untargeted conservation programs at Phoenix Water Services Department

	Emergency Retrofit	Retrofit	Depot	Audit
Inception Date	1985	1989–1990	1989	1996
Duration	2 years	3 years	current	1 year
Impetus	Emergency measure to reduce sewer flow	To implement 1986 Conservation Plan	Response to political concern over water rates	Conservation Plan
Goals	Emergency demand reduction, reduce sewer flow	Save water at low cost	Save water est. responsiveness to customer concerns	Save water
Design and Implementation Difficulty 1 = very easy 10 = very difficult	7	5	5	3
Program Modifications	Some	Some	Few	Many
Financing	Expensed	Expensed	WRAF, WW	WRAF, WW
Overall Program Effectiveness	9–10	9	10	1
Effectiveness in Saving Water	8	5	7–8	1
Customer Response	10	9	10	1

Source: Based on materials provided by Phoenix Water Services Department.

program used water-saving plumbing devices, such as low-flow showerheads and toilet-tank dams. The conservation plan included acquiring additional water supplies, increasing the water treatment and distribution system capacity as well as efficiency, and expanding the capability for monitoring water quality.[*]

Depot Program

The Depot Program began in 1989 in response to political concern over rising water rates. Its purpose was to save water as well as establish greater responsiveness to customer concerns. The program is a largely self-installed retrofit program. Customers pick up conservation materials

---

[*] Water Conservation Plan, City of Phoenix Water and Wastewater Department, July 1986.

for self installation. These materials include toilet-tank dams or hanging bags, as well as shower-heads and faucet aerators. Instructions for installing these items, as well as brochures on Xeriscape™ lawn watering and pollution prevention, are provided.

Audit Program

The Audit Program, beginning in 1996 and lasting 1 year, was based on the Conservation Plan. It intended to save water resources as well as maintain a cost-effective, reliable water supply. This mission was attempted through implementation of policies regarding water supply availability, as well as infrastructure and financing, construction, reclaimed water use, groundwater use and artificial recharge, water quality, development of new water resources, water-demand management, and other environmental considerations.[*]

Utility Rate Structure and History

Phoenix has a seasonal uniform rate structure that applies to all customer classes. The peak rate is applicable June through September; the off-peak rate is applicable December through March; and the mid-peak rate is applicable to the remaining four months. A block of usage is included in the monthly service charge.

A nonseasonal uniform environmental usage charge is also applied to all customers. The uniform rate is higher for outside-city customers than for inside-city customers. The peak rate exceeds the off-peak rate by 54 percent. Although conservation was an important objective, the rate structure was also influenced by criteria such as revenue sufficiency, efficiency, equity, public acceptability, and administrative feasibility.

The revenue requirements of Phoenix are determined on a cash basis, with cost allocation based on the base-extra capacity method, with the peak season rate targeted to estimates of long-run marginal cost. The PWSD sets wastewater rates, charging a uniform rate that varies by customer class. This uniform rate is applied to a percentage of the average January, February, and March usage for each customer.

---

[*] Phoenix Water Resources Plan, City of Phoenix, Water Services Department, Water Engineering Division, 1995.

The PWSD assesses the results of conservation rates, such as reduced peak demands and deferred capacity savings, as very important. It ranks reduced average demands, reduced operating costs, and reduced customer bills as being less important than peak-demand reductions. It ranks the problems of conservation rates, such as revenue instability, increased customer costs, and customer equity, as very important.

Although the rate structure departed from the previous rate structure, the initial response of the majority of customers was positive. However, apartment complex associations oppose the rate structure because the usage allowed in the service charge is per-meter and not per-residence; in addition, under the previous rate structure, multifamily residential customers were classified as commercial, thus paying a lower rate than residential.

The water rate structure was implemented in 1990. Since that time, studies have indicated that the rate structure has resulted in peak month demand reductions of 3.6 percent for single-family households. In addition, customers with large areas of turf have requested considerable conservation assistance, given the higher peak rate. In general, customers appear to be very aware of the seasonal variation in rates.

PORTLAND, OREGON, BUREAU OF WATER WORKS

Overview

The Bureau of Water Works for Portland, Oregon, supplied 38.9 billion gallons of water in 1996–1997.* A total of 775,000 people were served, with an annual per-capita consumption of 50,200 gallons, or 137 gallons per capita per day. In the same year, there were 156,900 retail customers, 17,900 commercial and industrial customers, and 41 percent of total consumption was to wholesale customers. Total water billings were in excess of $53 million. This information is summarized in Table A.6.

---

* Statistical-Technical Report FY 1996–1997, Bureau of Water Works, City of Portland.

Table A.6

Summary characteristics for City of Portland, Oregon, Bureau of Water Works

Population	800,000
Residential customers	140,000
Commercial and industrial customers	17,900
Amount of water supplied	38.9 billion gallons in 1996–1997
Annual per capita consumption	50,200 gallons (137 gallons per day)

Source: Based on materials provided by City of Portland, Oregon, Water Department.

History and Motivation

The Bureau's low-income program was motivated by a concern that increases in water and sewer rates were unduly burdening a segment of the population.[*] The combined sewer and water bills have increased at a rate faster than inflation, and this trend is expected to continue. Portland's combined rates are higher than the national average, with increases in water service bills being driven primarily by the sewer system capital improvements. The sewer system is an old combined overflow system. Sewer mains that were once creeks have been put under ground.

In absolute terms, the bills are considered affordable by common standards. Water and wastewater rates are well below the typical cited range of 1.5 to 4 percent of income. The motivating forces include the trend for rates to increase, along with expected increases and anecdotal evidence from local social service departments that have identified a subset of the population that reportedly is burdened by current rates.

Although the Portland area has had low unemployment (4.8 percent), this belies the distribution of income and secular trends in the regional economy. Although salaries in professional occupations have increased in recent years, average wages per worker have declined, pulled down by stagnation in low-paying service-sector jobs.[†] Most job growth is expected to occur in the low-wage range.

---

[*] Interviews with Bureau staff and *Financial Assistance Programs and Lifeline Rates* prepared by the Lifeline Rate Committee, June 1997.

[†] Portland Bureau of Economic Analysis, reported in *Financial Assistance Programs and Lifeline Rates* prepared by the Lifeline Rate Committee, June 1997.

Current Programs

Eligibility requirements for the current program have several components. First, eligible water service customers must pay their bill. Renters and multifamily residents are not eligible; the program is restricted to single-family homes. There is a system of minimum income requirements that, in fiscal year 1998–1999, limit adjusted gross income to $24,672 for a family of four.

The four components of the low-income program, summarized in Table A.7, include bill discounts, crisis assistance, fixture repair, and self-help workshops:

- The bill discounts include a 25-percent discount of an average low-income customer's quarterly bill. Currently the discount is capped at a maximum of $33.48; the average consumption is 500 cubic feet per month.

- Crisis assistance includes emergency payment vouchers that can be allocated to a customer for a maximum of $75 per 12-month period.

- Fixture repair for homeowners includes $500 for minor repairs and up to $1,000 for outdoor underground leaks or behind-the-wall pipe repairs.

- Self-help workshops have attracted 700 participants per year. The workshops cover how to detect leaks, minor repairs, water-reduction tips, and distribution of retrofit kits.

Table A.7

Summary of conservation programs at City of Portland, Oregon, Bureau of Water Works

	Bill discounts	Crisis assistance	Fixture repair	Self-help workshops
Inception date	1995			1996
Duration	Ongoing	Ongoing	Ongoing	Ongoing
Impetus	Burden of rate increase—combined water and sewer	Rate increases and economic conditions of poor	Low-income assistance and system leak integrity	Low participation
Goals	Reach low income	Alleviate temporary financial crisis	Help low-income customers with leaks	Accommodate self-reliant culture of many participants
Program modifications	Some	Some	Some	Many
Financing	Bureau of Water Works Budget and Rates			

Source: Based on materials provided by City of Portland, Oregon, Bureau of Water Works.

Several additional components of the Bureau's payment program are beneficial to low-income customers, although all customers are eligible for these programs: payment extensions, monthly billing, and interest and/or penalty write-offs.

Issues and Development

About 25,000 bill-paying participants were originally estimated to be eligible for the low-income program. The original program was budgeted for 10,000 participants. As of 1998, less than 4,000 bill payers have participated in the program. Three reasons have been cited for the lower-than-expected participation: some low-income customers never seek help, pride in not being on public assistance, and ineffective marketing. It is also suspected that the working poor do not have the time to fuss with water conservation because they must focus on income. The staff is considering a variety of strategies to enhance program participation, including marketing. The Bureau is part of the Coalition for Conservation, which works collectively to enhance conservation and serve the combined media market of 17 water providers in the region. Of the providers, only Portland has a low-income assistance program.

The program has been assessed and reported on at least twice since its inception. Reports were published in December 1996 and June 1997.[*] Recommendations generated in this process include extending the program to renters and multifamily residences.

ST. LOUIS COUNTY WATER COMPANY

Overview

The St. Louis County Water Company serves the area to the north, west, and south of the City of St. Louis, Missouri, in St. Louis and Jefferson Counties (excluding the city of St. Louis, which is served by the municipal water system). The area includes five wholesale customers as well as two with alternative water sources. The area receives approximately 26 inches of precipitation annually, although the actual rainfall was much higher in 1997 and 1998. The Water

---

[*] *Financial Assistance Programs and Lifeline Rates* prepared by the Lifeline Rate Committee, June 1997.

Company obtains 80 percent of its supply from the Missouri River and 20 percent from the Meramec River. Supplies of water here are considered plentiful. There are four treatment facilities with a total capacity of 401 million gallons per day. The St. Louis County Water Company has a service area of about 500 square miles, which includes 91 towns and villages as well as substantial unincorporated areas; the diverse population totals 1.2 million. The system has 340,000 service connections—approximately 277,596 single-family connections, 7,079 multifamily residential connections, 55,325 commercial and industrial connections, and some wholesale connections. The company pumped 57.9 billion gallons of water in 1996–1997 and supplied 49.1 billion with a per-capita consumption of 315 gallons per day (191 gallons per day in winter). This information is summarized in Table A.8.

Low-Income Programs

The utility does not have a low-income program. Customer service personnel refer people to churches and charitable organizations for assistance. Connection and disconnection costs are

Table A.8

Summary characteristics for St. Louis County Water Company

Region	Area north, west, and south of the City of St. Louis, Missouri, in St. Louis and Jefferson Counties
Annual precipitation	22.6 inches
Population served	1.2 million
Total number of customer accounts	340,000 connections
Single-family residential customers	277,596 connections
Multifamily residential customers	7,079 connections
Commercial and industrial customers	55,325 connections
Overview of water supply	Surface water: 80 percent Missouri River; 20 percent Meramec River
Consumption per capita	315 gallons per day (191 gallons in winter)
Overview of water demand	Fluctuates with precipitation but generally stable, sales between 1996 and 1997 grew 1.6 percent
Total system billed consumption for 1996–1997	49.1 billion (85 percent of water pumped)
Total system water production for 1996–1997	57.9 billion (pumpage)

Source: Based on materials provided by St. Louis County Water Company.

$38 each ($76 total). Because customers pay only $20 for reconnection, each episode costs the company $56. With older service lines, disconnection can cause a much more expensive problem, costing as much as $800 to repair; plumbing charges can vary dramatically and consumers can be overcharged.

Between 1996 and 1997, uncollectible accounts grew from $255,491 to $360,731. Customers must contact the company if they are having difficulty paying their bill. Over the years, the company's policy has evolved to empower customer service personnel to work with low-income households to find solutions that avoid disconnection. For example, customers might arrange to pay a portion of the amount owed on a monthly basis.

The company meters and bills customers quarterly. Tenants are not submetered or billed. In a recent informal customer survey, about one third of the respondents indicated interest in a budget-billing plan. Budget billing is perceived as potentially beneficial for fixed-income customers.

Conservation Programs

The company does not have a conservation program or plan. Water supplies and capacity historically have been plentiful, and costs and prices are relatively low. Little conservation-oriented information is provided to customers. Bills are mailed in envelopes (postcards are not used), so conservation-related information can be mailed with the bills.

Energy conservation programs are implemented by other local utilities. The St. Louis County area is served by AmerenUE and Laclede Gas. Both companies have voluntary $1 donation programs to help customers in need. AmerenUE implements Energy Plus, an umbrella of 18 programs designed to meet special customer needs. These programs include Dollar More, Customer Assistance, Weatherization Kits, Energy Wise/Energy Smart, and Energy Plus Grants (which specifically fund energy-efficiency projects that assist low-income customers).

Rate Structure

The Water Company implements a relatively simple uniform rate structure, billed quarterly for residential and most commercial customers and monthly for industrial and larger commercial customers (Table A.9). The minimum charge includes a water-usage allowance.

Table A.9

Rate structure for St. Louis County Water Company

Meter size (in.)	(AM) Monthly billing, 200 cubic foot water allowed	(AQ) Quarterly billing, 600 cubic foot water allowed	Prorated service charge (3)*
⅝	$ 8.75	$ 17.26	$ 6.54
¾	$ 9.43	$ 19.32	$ 7.56
1	$ 10.80	$ 23.42	$ 9.61
1½	$ 14.22	$ 33.67	$ 14.74
2	$ 18.32	$ 45.97	$ 20.89
3	$ 29.25	$ 78.78	$ 37.30
4	$ 41.55	$115.69	$ 55.75
6	$ 75.73	$218.21	$107.01
8	$116.74	$341.24	$168.52
10	$171.42	$505.27	$250.54
12	$226.09	$669.31	$332.56

Commodity charge

*For all water used as registered by the meter, above the water allowance, the commodity charge is $1.4459 per 100 cubic feet.

NOTE: Approved tariff in effect for St. Louis Country Water Company as of August 1998.

Interview Protocol

Confidentiality Statement

YOUR RESPONSES TO THE FOLLOWING QUESTIONS WILL BE TREATED IN COMPLETE CONFIDENCE AND USED ONLY TO EVALUATE CONSERVATION PROGRAMS IN YOUR SERVICE AREA. TO PROTECT THE IDENTITY OF RESPONDENTS, RESULTS OF THIS INTERVIEW WILL ONLY BE PRESENTED IN A SUMMARY FORM.

Interview Identification

Date of Interview: _____

Name of Organization: _____

Name of Respondent: _____ Job Title _____

Information to Collect Prior to In-Person Interviews

Service area descriptive statistics to be compiled prior to interviews for fact-checking and in preparation for development of assessment model:

State, region

Annual precipitation

Service area (square miles)

Population served (year of estimate and source)

Number of single-family residential customers

Number of multifamily customers

Number of multifamily dwelling units

Total system billed consumption for 1996–1997

Total system water production for 1996–1997

Consumption per capita

Description of utilities current rate structure (rate schedule and/or code)

Other demographics (income, age, race distributions)

Overview of water demand

Overview of water supply

Conservation program background:

    Program descriptions

    Rate schedule and code

    Program reports and other documentation

    Proposals to governing boards, meeting minutes

    Relevant planning documents

Utility rate structure and history:

    Definition of billing system indicators for low-income customers

    Procedures to verify and update status of low-income customers

Programs

Low-Income Programs

We are interested in the overlap between your conservation programs and low-income customers. Has your agency/district ever sponsored conservation programs that targeted low-income customers? If so, please list:

Are there other programs to assist particular target populations, such as the elderly, disabled, or other groups with special needs?

Overview of Conservation Programs

Has your agency/district ever sponsored untargeted conservation programs that still affected low-income customers? If so, please list:

What other conservation programs have been implemented?

Which programs were considered or developed but not implemented?

Do any of these programs indirectly target low-income customers?

For each defined conservation program, elicit the following information:

Program identifiers and timing

    Formal name of program

    Approximate date of the program's formal inception

    Duration

Staffing and organizational capabilities

    Were you personally involved in the creation of the program?

    Were you personally involved in the implementation of the program?

    Did this program involve significant additional effort on your part?

    If not you, then who did?

    What type of staff skills are needed to make these programs successful?

    What other organizational capabilities are needed?

    Were these skill and other capabilities available to your agency?

    If the program implementation was contracted out, what capabilities were needed to administer and oversee the work?

Motivation and background for existing programs

    Describe the circumstances that led up to the creation of the program.

    What was the political impetus behind the creation of the program?

    Were there other motivations for the development of the targeted programs?

    Who motivated the program development (agency, local political figures, customers)?

    Describe any cross-pollination with other water agencies.

Original program design and features

    Describe the program as originally designed.

    What are the goals of the existing programs?

    Were the existing programs difficult or straight forward to design and implement?

Modifications to program over time

    What changes were made to the program in the first year? After?

    How have existing programs been modified over time?

    What motivated the changes?

    Did the changes serve their intended purpose? Is the program better as a result? Are there additional program modifications that are being considered?

    What is the next phase of the program?

    Is there a need to continue the program over time?

Financing programs

    How were the programs funded?

    Was cost sharing involved with other agencies/sources (e.g., energy, wastewater, or welfare agencies)?

    What has been the program budget since its inception?

Rate impacts and incidence

    Was a rate adjustment necessary to fund the program?

    Have rates been implemented to assure revenue neutrality?

    Do rates provide efficient price signals? Whose rates have increased and whose have decreased?

Effectiveness assessment (strengths and weaknesses)

    On a 1-to-10 scale, how successful do you think the program was?

    What were the most important barriers to the program's success?

    What is your impression of the program's effectiveness in achieving water savings?

    In percentage terms, what level of water use reduction would you expect among participating customers?

    How confident are you in this estimate? Could you give a range of expected savings?

    Besides water savings, what additional benefits would you attribute to the program?

    Has the program been formally or informally evaluated?

Public relations

    What is your impression of your customers' response to this program?

        1 = very negative, 10 = very positive)

    How would you describe the public relations benefits from the program (if any)?

    Any public relations nightmares?

    What has been the response in the press?

    Other customer responses?

Lessons learned, advice to other agencies planning such programs

    What advice would you give to other agencies contemplating similar programs?

    What would limit the applicability of your program to other areas?

    What are the important lessons that you learned in the development and implementation of the program?

    What special features or design elements of the program are important for its operation and success?

Snowball Sampling Questions:

    Who else in your utility should I speak with on these questions? (name and numbers)

    Do you have any suggestions for individuals outside the utility who we should speak with? (name and numbers)

    Are there any additional questions that you wish I would have asked you?

REFERENCES

Albouy, Y. 1997. *Marginal Cost Analysis and Pricing of Water and Electric Power.* Inter-American Development Bank, Chap. 1, p. 23.

Allen, J., and D. Davis. 1993. Using Coupon Incentives in Recycling Aluminum: A Market Approach to Energy Conservation Policy. *Jour. of Consumer Affairs,* 27(2):300–319.

Amatetti, E.J. 1994. Managing the Financial Condition of a Utility. *Jour. AWWA,* 86(4):184.

American Water Works Association. 1992. *Alternative Rates, AWWA Manual M34.* Denver, CO: American Water Works Association.

Babcock, T.M. 1995. Unintended Impacts of Water Pricing Policies on the Very Low Income Consumer. *Proc. Conserv96.* Denver, CO: American Water Works Association. pp. 745–749.

Baker, C.D. 1995. Learning to be Water Wise and Energy Efficient, Youth Education Program. In *Proc. Conserve96.* Denver, CO: American Water Works Association. pp. 89–92.

Bamezai, A. 1997. Application of Difference-in-Difference Techniques to the Evaluation of Drought-Tainted Water Conservation Programs. *Evaluation Review,* 19(5):559.

Bauman, K.J. 1999. *Extended Measures of Well-Being: Meeting Basic Needs.* Current Population Reports. Washington, DC: U.S. Census Bureau.

Baumann, D.D., J.J. Boland, and J.H. Sims. 1984. Water Conservation: The Struggle over Definition. *Water Resources Research,* 20(4):428.

Baumann, D.D., J.J. Boland, and W.M. Hanemann. 1998. *Urban Water Demand Management and Planning.* New York: McGraw-Hill, Inc.

Beecher, J.A. 1994. Water Affordability and Alternatives to Service Disconnection. *Jour. AWWA*, 86(10):61–72.

Beecher, J.A., and P.C. Mann. 1990. *Cost Allocation and Rate Design for Water Utilities*. Columbus, OH: The National Regulatory Research Institute.

Beecher, J.A., P.C. Mann, Y. Hegazy, and J.D. Stanford. 1994. *Revenue Effects of Water Conservation and Conservation Pricing*. Columbus, OH: The National Regulatory Research Institute.

Bohne, D.L. 1995. Plumbers to People. In *Proc. Conserv96*. Denver, CO: American Water Works Association. pp. 765–769.

Box, G.E.D., and G.C. Tiao. 1975. Intervention Analysis with Applications to Economic and Environmental Problems. *Jour. American Statistical Association*, 70(349): 70–75.

Burns, R.E. 1994. *Alternatives to Utility Service Disconnection*. Columbus, OH: The National Regulatory Research Institute.

Caravajal, A. 1993. Bilingual Water Conservation Programs in California. In *Proc. Conserve93*. Denver, CO: American Water Works Association. pp. 1989–1992.

Chesnutt, T.W., A. Bamezai, C.N. McSpadden, J. Christianson, and W.M. Hanemann. 1995. *Revenue Instability and Conservation Rate Structures*. Denver, CO: American Water Works Association Research Foundation and the United States Bureau of Reclamation.

Chesnutt, T.W., and J. A. Beecher. 1998. Conservation Rates in the Real World. *Jour. AWWA*, 90(2):60.

Chesnutt, T.W., D.M. Pekelney, and M. Hollis. 1998. Why do you always tell me it depends when I ask you how big a sample I need: A primer on sample size calculations. *Proc. American Water Works Association Annual Conference*. Dallas, TX.

Chesnutt, T.W., C.N. McSpadden, and J. Christianson. 1996. Revenue Instability Induced by Conservation Rate Structures. *Jour. AWWA*, 88(1):52–63.

Chesnutt, T.W., et al. 1996. *Designing, Evaluating, and Implementing Conservation Rate Structures*. Sacramento, CA: The California Urban Water Conservation Council.

City of Phoenix. 1998. *Water Conservation Plan*. Phoenix, Arizona.

Day, M.D. 1993. Is Water Affordability a Pricing Priority? Presented at the Annual Meeting of the American Water Works Association, San Antonio, Texas, June 1993.

Dietz, C., and J. Ranton. 1995. Targeted Programming for Low Income Households. In *Proc. Conserv96*. Denver, CO: American Water Works Association. pp. 755–759.

Downs, P.E., and J.B. Freiden. 1983. Investigating Potential Market Segments for Energy Conservation Strategy. *Jour. Public Policy and Marketing,* 2:136–152.

Doxsey, N., and J. McNabb. 1998. *The Geographer's Craft*. Department of Geography, University of Texas at Austin. http://www.utexas.edu/depts/grg/ustudent/gcraft/fall97/mcnabb/final/program.html.

Durand, R., and R.C. Allison. 1995. Who are Citizen Water Conservationists? A Demographic Profile. *Water Management in Urban Areas,* (November):343–349.

Dziegielewski, B., and E. Opitz 1991. Municipal and Industrial Water Use in the Metropolitan Water District Service Area. As reported in Baumann, Boland, and Hanemann 1998, 67–72.

Edin, K., and L. Lein. 1997. *Making Ends Meet: How Single Mothers Survive Welfare and Low-Wage Work*. New York: Russell Sage Foundation.

Energy Information Administration. 1997. *Residential Energy Consumption Survey*. Washington, DC: U.S. Department of Energy.

Gallegos, P., and E. Hernandez. 1995. Denver's Low Income Conservation Program. In *Proc. Conserve96*. Denver, CO: American Water Works Association. pp. 761–764.

Iadarola, C., et al. 1995. Water Demand Management in Multi-Family Housing—The Role of Economics. In *Proc. Conserve96*. Denver, CO: American Water Works Association. pp. 959–963.

Lent, T. 1989. *Philadelphia Water Department Conservation Pilot: Final Evaluation*. Philadelphia, PA: Energy Coordinating Agency of Philadelphia, Inc.

Lifeline Rate Committee, City of Portland. 1997. *Report on Financial Assistance Programs and Lifeline Rates*. Prepared for the Portland City Council.

Little, V.L., and P.H. Waterfall. 1990. Make Every Drop Count in Commercial and Multi-Family Landscapes: A Cooperative Project Between the City of Tucson and the University of Arizona. In *Proc. Conserve90*. Denver, CO: American Water Works Association.

Martin, R.C., and R.P. Wilder. 1992. Residential Demand for Water and the Pricing of Municipal Water Services. *Public Finance Quarterly*, 20(1):93–103.

Metropolitan Water District of Southern California and the Los Angeles Department of Water and Power. 1991. *A Model-Based Evaluation of the Westchester Water Conservation Programs*.

Miller, M., et al. 1992. *Final Report on the Investigation of Uncollectible Balances, Docket No. I-900002*. Harrisburg, PA: Bureau of Consumer Services, Division of Consumer Research, Pennsylvania Public Utility Commission.

Mullarkey, N. 1991. Low Volume Toilets Retrofits in Two Low-Income Public Housing Projects. In *Proc. AWWA Annual Conference*. Denver, CO: American Water Works Association. pp. 487–495.

Nero, W.L., D. Mulville-Fiel, and D.L. Anderson. 1993. The Impact of Water Conservation Plumbing Fixtures on Institutional and Multi-Family Water Use: Case Studies of Two Sites in Tampa, Florida. In *Proc. Conserve93*. Denver, CO: American Water Works Association. pp. 1817–1830.

Nicholson, W. 1995. *Microeconomic Theory: Basic Principles and Extensions*. 6th ed. Fort Worth, TX: Dryden Press.

Pape, K.L. 1998. Affordability: A View from an Investor-Owned Utility. Presented at the Annual Conference of the American Water Works Association, Dallas, Texas, June 1998.

Park, J.L., and R.B. Holcomb. 1996. A Demand Systems Analysis of Food Commodities by U.S. Households Segmented by Income. *American Journal of Agricultural Economics*, 78(2):290–301.

Pekelney, D.M., and T.W. Chesnutt. 1997. *Landscape Water Conservation Programs*. A report for the Metropolitan Water District of Southern California.

Pekelney, D.M., T.W. Chesnutt, and W.M. Hanemann. 1996. *Guidelines For Preparing Cost-Effectiveness Analyses of Urban Water Conservation BMPs*. A report for the California Urban Water Conservation Council, Sacramento, California, September 1996.

Pekelney, D.M., T.W. Chesnutt, and D. Mitchell. 1996. Cost-Effective Cost-Effectiveness: Quantifying Conservation on the Cheap. *Proc. 1996 Annual Conference of the American Water Works Association*. Denver, CO: American Water Works Association.

Poch, X. 1995. Austin's Free Toilet Program: Cheaper than Rebates! In *Proc. Conserv96*. Denver, CO: American Water Works Association. pp. 649–653.

Pollyea, M.A. 1993. Conservation Assistance Program for Low Income Customers. In *Proc. Conserv93*. Denver, CO: American Water Works Association. pp. 1895–1898.

Rubin, S.J. 1994. Are Water Rates Becoming Unaffordable? *Jour. AWWA*, 86(2):79–85.

Saunders, M. 1992. Water and Sewer Rates—The Emerging Crisis for the Poor. In *Proc. Biennial Regulatory Information Conference.* Columbus, OH: The National Regulatory Research Institute, pp. 21–33.

Saunders, M., et al. 1998. *Water Affordability Programs.* Denver, CO: American Water Works Asociation Research Foundation.

Sutherland, R.J. 1994. Income Distribution Effects of Electric Utility DSM Programs. *Energy Journal*, 15(4):103–119.

Tollen, P. Not dated. *Affordable Water for Low-Income Customers: The Philadelphia Story.* Philadelphia Water Department.

U.S. Department of Agriculture. 1997. *Household Food Security in the United States in 1995: Summary Report of the Food Security Measurement Project.* Washington, DC: U.S. Department of Agriculture.

U.S. Department of Commerce. 1999. *Statistical Abstract of the United States 1998.* Washington, DC: U.S. Department of Commerce.

U.S. Department of Labor. 1997. *Consumer Expenditure Survey 1997.* Washington, DC.: Bureau of Labor Statistics.

U.S. Environmental Protection Agency. 1998. *Water Conservation Guidelines.* Washington, DC: U.S. Environmental Protection Agency.

Whitcomb, J.B., J.W. Yingling, and M. Winer. 1993. Residential Water Price Elasticities in Southwest Florida. In *Proc. Conserv93.* Denver: American Water Works Association. pp. 695–701.

ABBREVIATIONS

AFDC   Aid to Families with Dependent Children

AGI   adjusted gross income

AHH   A Helping Hand

AWWARF   AWWA Research Foundation

BWEC   Bureau of Water and Energy Conservation

CAADC   Community Action Agency of Delaware County

CAP   Central Arizona Project

ccf   hundred cubic feet

CCP   Community Conservation Partnership

CF   cubic feet

DEP   Department of Environmental Protection

DWP   Department of Water and Power

gpcd   gallons per capita per day

HSD   Human Services Department (City of Phoenix, Arizona)

LIURP   Low Income Usage Reduction Program

NEC   Neighborhood Energy Center

NHN   Neighbors Helping Neighbors

NPV   net present value

PAR	Program for Alternative Rates
PCAP	Pilot Customer Assistance Program
PSW	Philadelphia Suburban Water
PUC	Public Utility Commission
PWSD	Phoenix Water Services Department
PWWD	Phoenix Water and Wastewater Department
SHS	Seniors Helping Seniors
SSI	Social Security Impound
ULFT	ultra-low-flush toilet